THE POWER OF WHY: 27 MUSICIANS CAPTURED THE LEAD

GLORY ST. GERMAIN

GLORYLAND PUBLISHING

COPYRIGHT

info@UltimateMusicTheory.com
Compiled By: Glory St. Germain
Edited By: Wendy H. Jones and Lisa McGrath
Cover Design By: Glory St. Germain

DEDICATION

To my mother and father, who gave me the blessings of music lessons and taught me that music would be part of my life forever. Music is like breathing.

To my brother Bradley, who taught me that learning something new takes courage. You are my inspiration to always keep learning.

To my loving husband Ray, for sharing your beautiful voice with the world and inspiring me to always Dream Big. Thank you for our children and our great adventures to be continued...

I love you all.

CONTENTS

BE LIKE THAT TREE

Joanne Barker
Canada

I recently went on a seven-hour road trip to visit family, passing through some of the most scenic areas of Ontario, Canada. As I enjoyed the beauty of the fall colours, I noticed how there was always that one tree that seemed to stand out more than others. Why? What made it so special? What had it done differently than the other trees? As I thought about it, I began to see similarities between the trees that stood out and my own journey which has seen me take the lead many times. Trees do not decide to stand out. They get noticed. I believe that there are three things required to make that happen – proximity, resources and resourcefulness. While a strong genetic makeup is important, a tree that flourishes makes good use of its proximity to resources like water, nourishing soil and sunlight. It also requires its own kind of resourcefulness as it lays down its roots to search out those life sustaining resources.

Two trees of the same variety beside each other do not even thrive in the same way. One seems to grow bigger and healthier, with more vivid coloured leaves and denser shade while another seems sparser and drabber. Are we truly any different?

Like those trees, I did not set out to be noticed. When I started taking piano lessons, I had no dreams of playing piano in front of even a small crowd, let alone becoming well-known as a performer at area events, a church music director, and a musician for over 400 funeral services. I did not see myself serving as a worship leader, lay preacher, and guest speaker at other churches, or officiating at funerals. I did not imagine becoming a Breast Cancer Patient Spokesperson, yet I was asked to fulfill that role for four years on behalf of a large hospital foundation, speaking at events that raised millions of dollars. Thousands of women have had breast cancer, why did they ask me? Professionally, I had no aspirations of running a business. I wanted to become a schoolteacher, but complications following knee surgery ended my university studies. Teaching piano seemed like a good fit. My desire to give my students the best possible lessons led me to seek out training to become a group piano teacher. I soon found myself speaking at teachers' meetings, international conferences, and taking on leadership roles within the organization. I had always enjoyed composing but had no thoughts of ever hearing any of my compositions performed in public. After creating my hybrid music program, I began writing my own lesson materials. My compositions are now favourites of my students and are frequently heard at recitals. My role with *Ultimate Music Theory* was not something I went looking for. I knew of Glory St. Germain as we had both taught the same music program. After several years, we had the opportunity to meet in person. Glory saw something in my abilities and energies that led her to invite me to be the Games Creator and UMT Community Manager. Both roles have really added to my fulfillment both personally and professionally. During 2021, I was a panellist at four *Magic of Music* summits and was named an International Best-Selling Author in three of the *Power of Why* series books. I did not go looking for any of these opportunities, but they did come my way. Why?As I reflect on the reasons why, I can now see that I am like that one tree that stood out from the others. That tree did not set out to take the lead. Proximity, resources, and resourcefulness helped that tree thrive and stand out. The same applies to my journey. Living across the street from my first piano teacher is why I started playing piano in the first place. Without that first step, I am not sure how the rest would have unfolded. Proximity is what started my journey. Without the confidence I gained from performing in public, I would not have developed the poise to stand up and share my spiritual, personal, and professional thoughts with others. Sharing my breast cancer story was not uncomfortable as I was used to being at the microphone in front of large crowds and had already officiated at funerals for two family members. Speaking about breast cancer seemed easy after those experiences. Resources, including aptitude, lessons, and coaching helped my journey flourish. Aptitude is required; however, being resourceful is also required. It is one thing to have ability and take lessons, yet it is another to commit and follow through with six hours a day of practice. Software for writing music and coaching to learn how to write music, a sermon, or speech are all available, but those tools need to be implemented to be meaningful. Resources are nothing without resourcefulness.

The only "why" I cannot answer is why I was noticed. I did not set out to take the lead when I took my place at the piano, nor did I ask to stand at centre stage to speak at fundraisers, church services, funerals, or summits. Becoming an author was not in my scope of possibilities, but now I celebrate being a three-time international best-selling author.

Sometimes taking the lead has more to do with what others

see in us than our desire to be the lead.

Like those beautifully coloured trees, we go about living our lives and without knowing it, someone notices us and sees us serving in a role we did not envision for ourselves. Being open to new experiences and willing to step out of your comfort zone can bring about amazing opportunities.

As you journey along your path, be like that tree. Make use of your proximity, resources, and resourcefulness so you can weather the storms that come your way.

Trees experience extremes in weather. We experience extremes in life. My extremes have included five knee surgeries, hand and wrist issues, arthritis, and cancer. Despite those challenges, or maybe because of them, I have flourished.

Life can throw all sorts of challenges at you as you lay down your roots. It is up to you to deal with how you will face them. Do not think that you have less to offer than others. Find a mentor. Join organizations with like-minded people. Seek out quality professional development.

Do everything you can to thrive and stay strong. Most importantly, take the lead in your own life.

Be like that tree, so when the time comes, you will be ready to take the lead.

Author Bio:

Joanne Barker, Pianist, Piano & Theory Teacher, Composer and International best-selling Author in the *Power of Why* series. She operates a successful music studio in Southwestern Ontario, Canada and serves as a member of the Ultimate Music Theory Team.

https://ultimatemusictheory.com/about-ultimate-music-theory/

LEADING AS A FIRST RESPONDER TO HUMANITY

Suzanne Greer
USA

W hat makes a great leader? I believe a genuine leader is someone who walks the walk, not just talks the talk. They are a person of integrity and authenticity, one who follows through with what they say they will do. A great leader is one who leads through example, who is virtuous, confident, and not afraid to take risks or make mistakes. Most importantly, a leader is a guide who inspires another to become better, realizing potential not yet discovered. I am fortunate to have wonderful teachers and mentors in my life who inspired me to become my best and to follow my dreams.

It all started in my small hometown at the youthful age of five when I started Suzuki violin lessons. My mother was a violinist and created an environment of music in our home. Hours of listening and private and group lessons, which I frankly did not enjoy until the day Mom took us to a solo piano concert downtown at the local arts center. I sat in amazement as I watched the concert pianist walk onto the stage, take a bow, and sit down at the large, black, magnificent concert grand piano. I was mesmerized as I watched his fingers flow effortlessly across the keys, creating magical and breathtaking sounds. I have vivid memories of this concert, and I specifically remember emotions welling up inside of me that said, "Yes, this is what I will do for the rest of my life."

Piano lessons came shortly after. I took lessons with a neighborhood teacher who sat in the kitchen on the phone for most of my thirty-minute lessons. I loved music, and I loved piano. I disliked the lesson books and would go home to instead play by ear all the popular songs of the day. Dismayed and unmotivated by age eleven, I asked if I could quit both violin and piano. Mom and Dad agreed. I took a year off and, in the meantime, spent hours at the piano on my own improvising and playing by ear. Frustrated by my lack of progress, I requested piano lessons again. This time, Mom found MaryAnn Swallum, a piano preparatory teacher at a local private college.

MaryAnn was an incredible teacher, mentor, and friend to me from those early junior high school days and well into my adult life. MaryAnn was devoted to piano and teaching excellence at the highest caliber. She was passionate about piano and music and equally passionate about passing along what she knew. With MaryAnn's gentle yet demanding guidance, I went on to pursue a career in music. Not only did MaryAnn guide me in piano, but she guided me in life. She demonstrated perseverance, strength, and compassion in everything she did. I credit her for giving me a firm foundation, one that had been lacking before I started studying with her. On a deeper level, my piano study with her during high school gave me the strength to overcome drug and alcohol addiction.

Music has always been a reprieve from the outside world for me. Music transformed me and continues to do so to this day.

Those many hours of practice in my living room as a young teenager were my refuge. Time spent with the great masters like Bach, Beethoven, Mozart, and Chopin healed my soul and touched my spirit. You know you must follow your path in music when you can think of nothing else that you would rather do with your life.

The road has not been easy. I believe my path in music was my calling. However, I was filled with fear upon graduating from college with a Bachelor of Music degree in piano performance. In my senior year of college, I battled depression and anxiety, mostly due to the fear of the unknown and fear of my future. I never thought or believed that I was good enough. I shudder when I remember a time where I wished that my hands would stop working so I didn't have to pursue what I felt others thought was nonsense. I figured my degree would not yield a well-paying job and it was akin to getting a degree in underwater basket weaving. My devoted father who saved his money to send me to a superb liberal arts college would not be happy if I couldn't land a job.

I persevered somehow. My anxiety manifested itself in poor health. I lost a lot of weight and in March of my senior year, I suffered a fracture in my femur after falling on the ice. Several weeks of bed rest and no piano practice followed. Still, I pushed on and once I could play piano again, I prepared for my senior piano recital in the spring. I am thankful and grateful to my college professor, David Brunell, who gave me the courage to continue and mentored me through those difficult college years.

Fast forward to my life now. I am a successful, well-respected member of my teaching community. Through a willingness to serve and to continue to learn from others, I have volunteered in many music teacher organizations. I have served on many levels including as president for local and state music teacher groups, as well as at the national level. Serving in these capacities has given me many opportunities. I wrote a blog entitled "The Courage to Charge What You're Worth" that led to being featured in David Cutler's book, *The Savvy Music Teacher.* During Covid, I embraced the fact that students had more time to practice. I had many successes such as students winning prestigious local events.

Despite all these successes, I have recently realized the only person who really doesn't believe in me, is me. I am very grateful to Glory St. Germain, the author of the *Power of Why* series, who has helped me to believe in myself. She has challenged me to dig deep and develop a positive mindset, to overcome limiting beliefs and to develop a new belief that I am enough. I am capable. I am strong. I am an Elite Educator. Continually striving for something better, I will never stagnate. I must lead, teach, and stay in music even when it's just plain hard because teaching music is a noble profession. Why? We are *first responders* to the human condition. Inspiring my students and other teachers gives me purpose. The feelings of insecurity, the feeling that I am not enough, and the struggle of not being perfect are dissolving as I accept that I am human. Leading in music helps me find this humanity.

Author Bio:

Suzanne Greer is a pianist and artist teacher at MacPhail Center for Music. As a Nationally Certified Teacher of Music, she specializes in teaching Suzuki, traditional piano lessons, and music theory.

https://www.macphail.org/faculty/suzanne-greer/

3

THE SECRET SAUCE TO SUCCESS

Heather Revell
New Zealand

W hy did the secret sauce to success help me capture the lead?

Life as a part-time classroom music teacher was rocking along nicely. My classes were playing keyboards, moving and grooving with rhythm activities, completing theory knowledge work, and I even had a junior recorder choir. Then we heard our department head was leaving and a fresh ideas director was joining our staff. She was experienced in school bands overseas, concert bands, and all students from years 5-8 would be learning a woodwind or brass instrument in the new band programme. School number one. This was an exciting initiative and so preparations began for instrument hire, book purchases, and instrument allocations for our current year's 4-7 students to begin in the new year. The new year came, and it began. Every student was issued with an instrument and classes began with tooting; goosehonks and duckfarts were heard across the school. It was a hilarious start. In no time at all we were performing for parents and several teachers joined in on their clarinets and trumpets, saxophones, etc., too. It was incredible to be a part of such an innovative programme under such an experienced and passionate director; we were the first New Zealand school to have the band programme as regular music class rather than as an extra-curricular (afterhours) programme. I was not experienced in leading ensemble band work but was given many opportunities to step up to the plate and direct pieces with our bands. We developed a festival band with our advanced students, a concert band, a jazz band, and an all-in band. Several years passed, and we held many concerts, festivals, and workshops in the school. During the time I was there, the director and I took our thirty-six-piece Jazz Band on tour to Melbourne and participated in the Fringe Festival there, and we performed and ran workshops for students and teachers at several schools. What a blast. It was such a wonderful experience for our students, support parents, and me. While I was teaching at that school, my director had put my name forward to direct bands for a trust/privately run charity that offered music opportunities in schools which did not have the money or ability to offer such a programme. I was offered the job on her recommendation and began setting up and teaching the band programme in two schools. Schools number two and three.

After several years, I left the first school to teach in another private college that was closer to my home and began the same programme there for year 7-9 students. It was very exciting to get the classroom music band programme set up there. We continued to perform at annual festivals and events together with my first school and saw the programmes grow every year as I continued directing bands at the other two schools as well. School number four. As well as the classroom music band programme, I started a developing Jazz Band. Halfway through the first year, I personally invited students who had demonstrated commitment and made good progress to join. Our first performance would be at a school community event three months later. Could we do it? Of course, we could, and we did.The whole school community supported our first performance with accolades, amazement, and appreciation. The following year we headed off to four national jazz festivals. In preparation for that, three parents got on board and fully supported the band, organised uniforms and music stand bandannas, as well as food and transport, while I was able to focus solely on directing and further developing the bands abilities. At the first festival, we placed 2nd and received a silver award for our performance. That was a real boost to the morale of the students because they were all so very nervous. We received another silver award at the second festival. The third and fourth festivals were open and involved three performances over the weekend events in different locations where people could come and hangout and listen.

At the same time as all this was going on in school number four, I developed a community Jazz Band with kids from schools two, three, and four. We rehearsed on weekends; I taught those students every week at their schools, and we set off for some performance opportunities at festivals too. It was so exciting to have students from all walks of life and economic backgrounds working together, building friendships, and supporting each other so well in the name of making music. We toured around New Zealand and greater Sydney on several occasions playing at schools and festivals alike. We also took part in annual festivals with school number one.

A decade or so later, I moved out of the city to enjoy a rural lifestyle. I began teaching bands in schools numbers five and six. And away I went on another journey to collective music making with students from year 3-13. I taught students privately and developed a jazz band in each school plus performances, training, community events, festivals and more.

I guess what I am really wanting to share here is how a seven-year-old beginner piano student trained as a qualified piano teacher and became a classroom music teacher with a BA in Music and Education. Furthermore, how she transitioned into a Band Programme Leader and Director, who then blossomed as a competent Band Director with a keen jazz interest. I played several instruments in the bands when we performed, and I learnt so much along the way. Who could imagine that I had started out with so little and ended my school music teaching career on such a high? Not me. From a follower to a leader. From a novice to a master (well mistress actually, ha-ha)

What was it that helped me make the transitions over the years and be able to develop my career and the abilities of my students, their engagement, and their excitement through making music together?

Why was I successful? How did I do it?

The Secret Sauce: I was teachable.

I believe that when we remain teachable, we are open: open to new ideas, new concepts, new strategies, new people, and new opportunities.

You will be blessed if you remain teachable too.

Author Bio:

Heather Revell is a Music Education Specialist who has over 20 years experience teaching privately, community and in schools in New Zealand. She is passionate about guiding her students on their musical journeys and supporting music parents.

https://musicwithheather.com

4

EMBRACING MY ALL-ENCOMPASSING
LIFE AS A MUSICIAN

Pam Turner
USA

B eing a musician defines who I am: I teach piano, compose
music, and serve as a church pianist. This also means I am
a small business owner, and I'm very proud of that. No one
cares as much about my work as I do, so I prefer to do things
myself without having to defer to someone else. I handle everything from writing the music, publishing and marketing, to
shipping books, while teaching piano, recording, and playing at
church in between. I can't always say that I feel like I've
captured the lead, but I can say that I've published nineteen
piano books, recorded eight albums - two of which are
streaming on Spotify, iTunes, Amazon, and various other sites -
and I think I've been a positive influence in the lives of my
students. I won the Sheet Music Plus Holiday Arranging
Contest in 2017 with "Christmas Medley", and I have several
titles listed in the current NFMC (National Federation of Music

Clubs) bulletin. I've participated in several online conferences with internationally recognized teachers and composers, and I'm always honored to be included with such great talents. I also try to recognize and appreciate my own abilities and do my best to maximize them. I'm all in as a musician, but my biggest hope is that I'm able to touch lives in a meaningful way through my music.

Most days, I don't think about what I've already accomplished; I think about what I have yet to accomplish, and that's what inspires me. My best advice to you is to keep at it. When you're tired or discouraged, when your sales aren't where you want them to be, when you're out of ideas, when you want to give up – keep at it. I'm a slow and steady wins the race kind of girl. I pace myself, but I work hard and always have another goal in sight.

What does it take to get there? Simple – follow your dreams. This is the idea behind the song I wrote, "Always Dream" based on Psalm 37:4, included in my Scripture Meditations book. A number of years ago, while still in another career, I said to myself, "I want music to be my life," and once I said that, it didn't take long for it to happen. I think we're all happier when we follow our passions, provided they're truly our destiny and not just a way to make money or impress people. If you're serious about your dreams, you'll pursue them relentlessly. I don't mean marketing your products till everyone is sick of them, and I don't mean mirroring someone else's work as a shortcut. Mentors and role models can be helpful but find your own way and be you.

It has taken me many years to be comfortable with being me. I had to work my way through decades of having significant people in my life belittle and criticize me. I was devalued to the point of literally having no self-esteem. Although this was a huge obstacle, there is something within me that keeps going. The current status of my work is a culmination of a long process, overwhelming sometimes because I have to stretch myself, but I'm very happy with where I am today.

At times, I look to the past and realize that my experiences were preparing me for today, both musically and as a businessperson. Teaching has given me a good understanding of people and their personalities and emotions. Being a church pianist has helped me develop improvisation skills, which is beneficial in composing and arranging. Being an executive bank officer and handling the bank's website gave me the knowledge to build and maintain my own website, complete with e-commerce and an overall appearance that I love. Banking also gave me experience with cash flow analysis and a multitude of other things. My love of photography, which started in childhood, led to learning creative editing, which is useful with marketing materials and sheet music covers. Whatever skills you have picked up during the course of your life, you will use as a small business owner.

As a business owner myself, I can say that one of the greatest assets you can have is the ability to learn. I've solved many problems by Googling or watching YouTube videos, whether it's something to do with notation software or mastering and distributing my recorded music. Keep an open mind, be ready to try something new, and be willing to develop the necessary skills to make things happen, whether that means taking a course or just doing some research.

As for my music, there is just something about it that reaches people. The majority of my writing is in the sacred genre, and people of faith can relate to it. Some say it's the expressive way I write, some say it enhances their own personal worship time, some say their congregations love it, and one teacher shared with me that her adult student was moved to tears when she played and sang along with my book of hymn arrangements.

I feel humbled by the fact that I've sold sheet music and

books all over the world and that I've been an active musician for as long as I have. My sales, my many years of teaching, composing, and playing at church are tangible, measurable achievements, but I'm equally proud of the little moments that I tuck away in my heart, such as when the parent of a student I had for ten years said, "You were more than a piano teacher, when a student of eight years who just started high school entered her online lesson visibly upset and felt comfortable enough to tell me about it, when a teacher friend played one of my songs for her little granddaughter who was having trouble falling asleep and the granddaughter wanted to hear it again, when someone at my church approaches me after the service and says, "I love to hear you play," when a stranger purchases sheet music and sends a heartfelt email that says, "I love your music." these are the things that are validating for me and provide the real evidence that I have found my place. I am not the best or the brightest in the music world by any means, but I am becoming what I was meant to be.

Author Bio:

Pam Turner is a piano teacher, church pianist, and composer. Sacred music is her passion, and she writes both arrangements and original pieces. She currently resides in Varnell, Georgia with her husband, dog, and three cats.

www.pamturnerpiano.com

5

WHEN THE MAGIC HAPPENS

Mike Reno
Canada

M usic has been in me for a very long time. I started out as an eleven-year-old boy who bought my first set of drums with money I earned from my morning paper route in Victoria, BC. I was one of the lucky ones who grew up with a great brother who always looked out for me.

He played guitar so I decided to play the drums. This started my musical adventure. My brother Steve was the guitar player and lead singer and he taught me how to sing back up and harmony. Boy did that ever come in handy.

When growing up in Victoria, my older brother told me that we should make our own money and then he proceeded to show me how. After my morning paper route and after school, Steve would take me downtown to a place where we could buy the afternoon paper, *The Times* for five cents. We would then stand in front of The Bay department store and yell at the top of our lungs, "Times paper," and read out the headlines of the day, it really worked. Many customers would flip us a quarter and say keep the change.

I'm thinking now it was probably because they thought I was a cute kid working hard. That's just one example of how my big brother took care of me. He's gone now but what a guy. He would always tell me that it's good to have a little walking around money.

That's how it all started, but now I'm going to skip ahead to the story I really wanted to share. After going out on my own, I found myself fronting bands, meaning I stood out front and sang the songs and entertained the crowd. This didn't come easy being a drummer/singer, but after a while, I got the hang of it.

After I finished high school, it was time to get serious about my music, so I headed to Calgary, Alberta to find some guys to start a band. It took a while, but I was now a lead singer in a band, no drums this time, and after a little practise, we became one of Calgary's top bands. Now, as it is with most new things, we didn't have a lot of money. So, when we weren't playing, we rented some PA equipment from the local music store. We then proceeded to dismantle the PA and take all the measurements. After we had written down all the measurements, we re-assembled the PA and returned it to the music store the next day. We had a little money put away to buy some wood and screws and we built our own PA system from scratch.

And to be a little different, we painted it bright orange. This was the only way a new group could ever afford a PA system. But we did it. Another example of getting 'er done. The group I'd formed picked a rather questionable name (Spunk). I know, right?

In Alberta in the early 70's there were bands playing six nights a week. This created a high level of competition and Spunk was number one on the provincial circuit. After creating a comfortable living after five years, I was offered an amazing opportunity which came out of nowhere. Turns out a band from Toronto had lost their singer and was looking across Canada for a replacement. A local promoter threw my name in the hat and after a brief audition, I got the job. The band in Toronto had done two relatively successful albums and wanted to record a new one. This was a huge opportunity for me. Trouble was I'd have to leave the Calgary band I'd started 5fiveyears earlier.

I was torn but decided to go and see what developed in Toronto. Little did I know that they would be leaning on me to write all the songs and front the new band. A big ask. I honestly don't know how I did it as I was not a song writer yet. They didn't know that, and I pretty much just faked it and ended up writing every song on their new album. This started my song writing career. After a few years playing with them, I wanted to do things that the band didn't. This caused me to leave the band and Toronto and head on an adventure that took me on a search for something better.

Shortly after this, when I was twenty-four years old, I found myself at a crossroads. My plan was to drive to Los Angeles and once again hook up with my brother. I needed to see what was happening in the California music scene. I didn't know exactly how it was all going to come together, but I headed out to Calgary to drop my girlfriend off for her new semester at University of Calgary and stay there for a few weeks before the big trip.

Little did I know that one winter night in Calgary, after a concert at a nightclub featuring Johnny Rivers, the plan started to develop. Upon leaving the nightclub through the back door, I crossed the alleyway to my car when I heard some noise coming from an abandoned warehouse. For some reason I poked my head in the small half door to the warehouse and in the middle of this huge empty space was a guy playing away on his guitar -

all by himself and playing a groove that sounded very hypnotic. Just then, he turned to me and invited me in. His name was Paul Dean and as it turns out he had just been let go from the band he started years earlier for apparently no good reason. When I look back on this moment, I realize that this was the exact moment I'd been searching for.

Paul and I would write two songs that night, and it was the start of what I can proudly say has been a forty-three-year long friendship and collaboration that started the band Loverboy. The reason I tell this story is because sometimes in life you have to look deeper, ask questions, and keep searching for what it is you really want. This friendship has produced many hit songs and many great memories of worldwide concerts, and it all happened because I wanted more. And I went looking for it. That's the lesson. Never give up searching for what your heart is trying to find. You never know when and where you find it until you find it. So, keep learning and keep writing and keep searching... It's there.

Author Bio:

Mike Reno is the lead singer and songwriter for the iconic 80's rock band, Loverboy. Over 10 million albums sold, 4 multi-platinum plaques, and a trio of double-platinum releases: Loverboy, Keep It Up, and Lovin' Every Minute of It.

www.loverboyband.com

6

BE ONE WITH YOUR SHADOW

Benny Ng
Australia

D o you accept yourself? I mean, truly accept yourself? Is there a part of you that you have cast aside because it does not fit the way you want to see yourself? Are there some negative qualities you have that you do not acknowledge? Carl Jung, renowned Swiss psychiatrist, called this the "shadow". He said: "Unfortunately there can be no doubt that man is, on the whole, less good than he imagines himself or wants himself to be. Everyone carries a shadow, and the less it is embodied in the individual's conscious life, the blacker and denser it is." How does this relate to being a musician? I will tell you in a bit.

When I discovered music, it was the era of cassette tapes and the Walkman. Listening to music using earphones was a novelty back then. Having only been listening to music through speakers, it was an amazing feeling to be immersed in the cacophony of sounds using such a small device. Homework time became something I looked forward to because I would have my earphones in the whole time. The soundscapes vibrating my adolescent eardrums stirred something in my soul. It opened a portal to another world.

High school was a treacherous time for me. I was from a middle-class family and most of my school mates were from the upper class. I felt isolated and ignored as the rift between my peers and I grew day by day. As I withdrew into my mind, I was trapped in a situation that took a huge toll on my mental health. I would look calm on the surface but pent-up emotions were boiling underneath that facade.

Music became my savior. Although I did not start making music until much later in life, listening to music gave me a release. Being a Capricorn, I am a detail-oriented person who treasures structure and creativity.

During my teenage years, I always thought I would become the next Bill Gates. I would immerse myself in the world of coding and make computer programs for Windows PC. Coding gave me the pleasure of working with mathematical details and structured algorithms. However, I did not feel like my creativity was stimulated the way I wanted it to be. I decided my calling was in another field, so I parted ways with computer programming.

Off to drama classes I went, hoping it would give me a fresh, exciting direction in life. Acting was fun and stimulating, but it lacked the autonomy over my own creations. More soul-searching was done before I opened my eyes to what was in front of me the whole time.

Music.

Music lets me dwell on details when I need to find the right rhyme, the right chord or the right note. It gives me immense satisfaction to comb through the thesaurus looking for the perfect word, to improvise on the piano looking for the catchiest melody, to strum all variations of the G minor chord in search for the ideal chord color.

Music demands an attention to structure because that is how people can make sense of the music they are listening to. Each word, melody and verse need to appear in a certain order to fulfil their purpose in a song. Music stimulates my creative juices when I sit down with a guitar and let words and melodies flow out of me.

My favorite band, Linkin Park, combined rock with many different genres of music, including electronic music. They would engineer their own sounds for their music. This captivated the technology geek in me. Sound design adds a whole new creative dimension to the art of song writing and production. Most of all, music allows me to express my innermost thoughts and emotions in a therapeutic way.

Other creative arts allow you to do that too, but music lets me express my thoughts and emotions with my voice. Given that the voice is deeply connected with the psyche, that is as intimate as it gets for me. I chose rock as the main genre I write for because I gravitate towards writing sad and angry songs. Being able to incorporate metal-style screaming into my music is a blessing because I feel empowered when I scream.

When writing songs, I draw from a well of life experiences that came mainly from my tumultuous high school years. There is a wonderful catharsis that comes from fleshing out those experiences and turning them into words and music. It helps me to confront and accept my "shadow self". I can finally make peace with my past and move forward with a renewed sense of purpose.

On a grander scale, I hope it helps to normalize mental health issues. For far too long, those issues have been considered a taboo topic. People have been suffering needlessly in silence for fear of what other people may think of them. What were my darkest thoughts would now be a beacon of hope to the listeners of my music?

I want my music to give others sanction to express their sadness, anger and anxiety. I want people to feel less alone and that it is normal to have negative emotions. It is okay to not be okay. It is only through accepting those emotions that we can manage them in a healthy way.

Music is the perfect vehicle to effect that paradigmatic change. And I want to be the catalyst.

Author Bio:

Benny Ng is a rock vocalist/songwriter who releases melodic rock music as Shadowary. He wants his music to give others sanction to express their emotions. Get unreleased music at shadowary.com

https://www.shadowary.com

7

CAPTURING THE LEAD

Mark Pfannschmidt
USA

W hat does it mean to "Capture the Lead"? When asked to write about this, my initial thought was: Capturing the Lead? Is that something I've done? Yet, as a teacher, I am a leader by definition, and I've worked hard to develop skill and continue learning so I can help my students more. But how did I get to where I am today?

Here's my story...

Since I was little, I've always loved music and wanted to be a musician. Since my early teens, I'd always quickly captured the lead among my violinist peers; the one thing I wasn't going to do was teach. I held the arrogant opinion–those who can play, do, and those who can't, teach. But after college, I quickly realized I was competing in a different league as a performer. I was getting some freelance work, but I lacked the dedication required to successfully audition for a full-time orchestra. Then within one week, two of my orchestra colleagues won auditions out of state and they called me to see if I could take over their students. My response to the first one, "I don't teach." When the second one called, I asked, "Who told you to call me?" The response, "Judy." So, I called my dear friend and colleague, Judy Silverman, and said, "What are you doing? I don't teach." I will always remember her response, "Mark, it's not rocket science, and besides, you'd be good at it. They already have books, just use what they have." I had been looking for a way to make more money as a musician. And so, my teaching career was born—no pedagogy training or background in teaching, just a solid understanding of how to play and a desire to help.

By the end of my first year, my lack of training had caught up with me. I felt like a fraud. So, I turned to Judy again and asked for advice. She referred me to Ronda Cole, who lives in my area and is an internationally known Suzuki teacher trainer. I took several of her classes and began to see how she systematically developed a solid technique which promoted musical expression, as well as how to build a program. I watched her teach for several months. The way she communicated with these children had a profound impact on my own teaching style. As I learned, I also realized that much of what I had been teaching was actually quite solid--I just didn't know what to expect. For example, I remember making the comment at one class, "This week is bow thumb week in my studio." She replied, "Bow thumb week? You mean bow thumb year." I didn't yet really understand that it takes time to develop good habits.

As a result of my friendship with Ronda, I got to know many Suzuki teachers in the area and had my own Suzuki program-- complete with private lessons and group classes. But at the end of three years I thought, "If I have to listen to another Bach Minuet, I'm going to scream." I was at a crossroads.

At that time, Rebecca Henry, another well-respected violin pedagogue, came to The Peabody Conservatory of Music. I took her violin pedagogy course and learned new practice techniques to remediate problems my students had and help them develop their technical and musical ability. Her systematic approach to teaching was fun, engaging, and physiologically sound.

I have always been someone who is looking for new pieces to play and teach, so I talked with colleagues and scoured area music stores for materials. I entered my students in local festivals and listened to the students of colleagues and was inspired to continue my growth as a teacher. My students started to place well in local competitions and began to audition successfully for local youth orchestras.

Finding my niche as a teacher has been a journey. Initially, I wanted to be a sought-after, world-class teacher, just like Ronda and Rebecca. I continued my training and started a DMA program. In the middle of my first year, I realized I didn't want to teach in a university, so I dropped out after that year. I had learned some important lessons about my personal limitations and had a chance to explore career options that were not right for me. But the more important questions lingered: Why do I want to be a teacher? What lights me up?

As I talked with my colleagues, I began to realize I especially enjoyed teaching students who had "problems." Some didn't perceive pitch well, or had serious rhythm problems, or had big gaps in their technique. Developing a strategy to fill in the gaps was engaging for me. I also had many who didn't practice regularly. I was honest with them about my own struggle in this area. I would tell them, "If there was a way to get better without practicing, I would have found it -it doesn't exist. I don't like to practice either, but I don't like to play badly."

I had finally found my Why. I wanted to teach because I wanted to help students overcome obstacles and succeed. They learned to practice better and do things they couldn't do before. More than three decades later, it still makes my day to see a student finally understand how to count a dotted quarter note, shift with a smooth motion, or develop the beginnings of a good vibrato. They understand how to move their fingers to match the symbols on the page. They've learned to notice what is on the page and what is not, and how to make musical choices with an understanding of the style of the period.

While I enjoy performing, both as a violist and as a pianist, I am most blessed to be a teacher. My life is so much richer because of my students and their families. They have brought me so much joy, and they are the reason why I continue to teach today. I've come a long way from that twenty-year-old who was not going to teach–indeed, I've captured the lead through teaching.

Author Bio:

Mark Pfannschmidt, BM, MM, UMTC is an RCM certified teacher. He teaches viola, violin and music theory. He and his wife, Laura, are the parents of two adult children, Jason and Emily.

https://www.MarkPf.com

8

LEADING THE VISION OF MUSIC

Rachel Dunn
Australia

I encourage you to look beyond what you can see, as the music industry has many hidden facets to explore.

My introduction to music came at a young age when I was growing up in the 1970s. I was carted around in the back of an Aussie Ute (a pickup truck) and squashed in next to the guitar amp driving from band practice to gigs.

My dad had a rock band in the country town I grew up in; this was my introduction to music. Dad also worked in a piano store, so it was natural to send me to piano lessons.

What a big mistake that turned out to be. I hated the piano. Not because of the sound but because I had the worst, most impatient, old-fashioned teacher. She was the best in town for classical prodigies, but she had her work cut out trying to teach a rebellious child who loved pop and rock music. I dreaded going to see her every Saturday morning.

This lesson has made me realise the importance of creating fun and encouragement when teaching.

If my piano teacher had given me more encouragement or looked at other kinds of music to teach me - something like the song Locomotive Breath by Jethro Tull - then who knows where I would be now.

I didn't have the musical ability that perhaps my family hoped for. In the end, after two years of frustration, my teacher told my dad he was wasting his money sending me to lessons, so my music career lay dormant.

That was until Dad purchased a record store. As a fifteen-year-old teenager, this was a dream come true. I worked part-time in a record store, met famous musicians, and was surrounded by great music.

That's when I started to notice music videos. I would stay up late and watch music videos every Friday and Saturday night. I became obsessed with the visual art of making music videos. I was fascinated by what made a good video and what made a great video. I daydreamed about what it would be like to make music videos myself.

I will never forget the day I decided to become a music video director. I was sitting on my white plush carpet, looking at a list of career options as a sixteen-year-old and listening to my *Hits of Summer* cassette. There was a long list of creative roles, and the word cinematographer grabbed my attention. I had no idea what the word meant at the time, but it grabbed me. So, I started looking into the film industry and started learning about directors. It was like the word lit up on the page, and from the moment it caught my eye, I knew my life's mission.

It was then I decided to follow my dream until it happened. I had no idea how I would get there, but I was determined to make it happen.

I want you to remember I grew up in a small country town with no media studies or film school. I had no mentors to help and no Google in those days. Everyone I went to school with wanted to be a mum or a teacher, maybe a doctor. From that moment on, I was obsessed with music videos. I did work experience at the local TV station but then, for my final year of school, we moved to a larger city. I was so excited to see Media Studies as an option at school. There were only three students in my class. I used the time to film my first music video using an old VHS camera. My teacher was so impressed and said that in thirteen years of teaching, he had never seen a student as driven and passionate as I was to create films. From there, I started working in the TV industry. I worked from the bottom up in every area. I thought this would make me a better director by learning all the facets of the profession. It was tough getting a break as a female director at that time. No matter how hard I worked, I found it very tough to get a break. I am still shocked to learn that only 5% of directors in Australia are women even now; female directors are still a rarity in the industry.

It wasn't until I moved to Sydney things started to ramp up in my career. I had a feeling that if I wanted to be the best, then I had to move to the biggest city I could to get my break. After finding the music video contacts, I stepped into my fears and approached people. I started getting jobs directing well known Australian artists until I was directing for some of the biggest stars of the time.

It's important to take time to acknowledge snapshots in your life. I will never forget the memory of sitting on a crane next to the cinematographer in 2001, directing a song called "Shine" by Vanessa Amorosi, when I felt pure happiness. I thought to myself, I made this happen. I am living out my dream, directing music videos, and I love it. I was so happy. Every part of me loved being on location, working with a team, and working together to bring an idea to life. It wasn't an easy ride to get there. It took risks, making mistakes, learning big lessons and never letting go of my vision. I kept directing bigger and bigger budgets and ended up leaving the TV industry. My husband Michael and I created a global business called Girl Director Academy.

We help people worldwide transform their confidence and make videos that stand out and help them create powerful, thought-provoking content to position themselves as an authority.

Using music in video content is something most people don't think about consciously when talking about video, but it is such an important part. Music inspires me to create; music sets the tone and can direct the emotion of the viewer.

The music video background has given me a depth to video in new and different ways most people don't even realise.

I believe today, learning how to evoke emotion with your viewer and being able to communicate using music with video is one of the most valuable skills you can learn as a business owner today. There are so many exciting paths you can take when it comes to music. I hope this inspires you to dream big, follow your quiet voice inside, and if it doesn't exist, create it.

Author Bio:

Rachel Dunn is a visionary with her ideas and creativity. Rachel and her husband Michael teach people to master video marketing inside their Girl Director Academy and are in post-production for their first documentary, "Through Elephant Eyes."

https://www.facebook.com/GirlDirector

9

A JOURNEY WITH MANY

Janet Olsen
United States

G rowing up, I knew music would always be an important part of my life. I grew up listening to all sorts of music. Singing and dancing filled my home and even though nobody was formally musically educated, we loved exploring new genes.

My musically inclined friends took piano, guitar, and voice lessons; they would go to a variety of shows and symphonies. It never bothered me as a young child because at home we were exposed to opera, Broadway, instrumental, and all sorts of works. The only difference was that my exposure was provided by the videos, records, and tapes available at our local library

As time went on, I also wanted to take music lessons and go to live shows like my friends. I quickly realized that those activities would be far from my reach. However, my father was determined to find an arrangement that would make me happy while not pulling on his wallet too much. To my delight, for

Christmas, I received a keyboard to start me on my musical journey. Unfortunately, the keyboard didn't include formal lessons. My 'teacher' was going to be my uneducated mother.

My mother lost her family when she was sixteen and cared for her younger sister without much help. She found her happy place when she heard music, so she started singing as therapy. One day someone brought her a newspaper clipping where auditions were to take place for the national choir of her country. Her friends at the house where she lived all encouraged and convinced her to audition even though she had never had any training.

She didn't know what an audition would be like or that she needed to prepare a piece. So, when the audition committee asked her to sing, she did with the only song she knew – "Silent Night". She had a beautiful voice, passed the ear training portion but couldn't read music and had no theory background. To her amazement, she was asked to join and spent years singing and learning in the National Choir of her country. And so, with the little she knew, I began my musical learning.

Assumptions can come back to bite you if they are wrong. My middle school teacher, Mr. R, didn't give me the time of day. I made many attempts to have him notice me. I volunteered, stayed after school, etc., but no matter how hard I tried, he would always skip me, ignore me, or act like I didn't exist.

I was starting to get desperate for him to interact with me. After all, he was the most popular teacher in the school, and I was going to need his help and recommendation if I wanted to get accepted into the prestigious arts school for entry to which everyone was preparing to audition.

One day, I stayed after class putting music away in the back room when I heard him talking to a group of students who were also auditioning for the music program at the arts school. He was laughing with them, giving encouragement, and scheduling audition preparation time with them. The room suddenly got quiet, and I heard him ask if anyone knew if I was auditioning. Some knew that I really wanted to, so they responded with a "Yes." He started laughing and said something to the effect of, "She's wasting her time, there is no way she will ever get in." My heart was crushed. I couldn't believe he would say that in front of my peers. Why was he saying that? Why would my teacher say that?

I spent the following week at my local library researching what an audition was and how to prepare for it. I listened to various artists singing the song I had chosen. I watched many dance routines and practiced in front of the TV. The audition was overwhelming, two rounds of vocal, dance, drama, theory, and interviews. It was a whole day affair with what looked like 500 kids. At every round there were less kids and somehow my confidence would increase a little each time I made it through a round.

After sitting on pins and needles for a few weeks, the letter came in the mail. To my amazement, I made it. I read and re-read the letter just to make sure I was reading and under-standing correctly. I checked that it was addressed to me, and I even had my father call the school to ask if the letter came from them.

My relationship with Mr. R ended officially on that day. I never went back to his music class, dropped out of all the choirs, and never spoke to him again.

Throughout the years I have thought back about this experi-ence. When I first started teaching, I promised myself that I would never make any of my students feel the way I did. They would never hear negatives about themselves come out of my mouth, and I would do my best to help them in any project or goal they may have. I would be their cheerleader and be with them every step of the way.

I grew up wanting to have experiences and opportunities like most of my peers. We weren't poor but we didn't have the money for all the extras my peers took for granted. There weren't brand clothes, sports, dance, or music lessons. We didn't go to the movies or eat out. Our car was a little older and we couldn't afford a house. Many avoided us and wrote us off, but throughout my life there have been many angels blessing me and helping me on this journey by cheering me on in my difficulties and in my triumphs.

Over the years, my studio has welcomed students from all walks of life: those with and without money, non-English speakers, disabled students and those with mental illness. I have learned from every one of them. When I walk into my studio every day, I take a minute to look at my degree, diplomas, and certifications. I don't just see my name on them but the names of all of those wonderful teachers, mentors, friends, and others who all had a part in helping me be the person I am today, as I serve on the State board of the Utah Music Teachers Association, am a Royal Conservatory of Music Center Representative, and an Ultimate Music Theory Elite Educator. I give them all a smile and start my day with them in mind.

Author Bio:

Janet Olsen is a classically trained pianist, vocalist and pedagogue. Fluent in English and Spanish, she specializes in piano pedagogy, music theory and the teaching of students on the Autism Spectrum. Currently residing in the USA, she and her husband are parents of 4 children.

www.facebook.com/janetolsenpianostudio

10

STRUGGLING TO GET MUSIC

Thulane Akinjide-Obonyo
Zimbabwe

I was really scared. I was five years old when Ms Eleanor Hizer asked me to play "Twinkle, Twinkle Little Star" on the piano. I could barely get the notes out. That was the start of a journey. A journey in taking the lead as a saxophonist, in a small town called Mutare, in Zimbabwe.

Fast forward seven years and I was crying on the basketball court at Peterhouse Girls School, the site where we had our annual Musicamp. I was twelve and the best recorder player in the country, but against these people, it did not matter. Five years of recorder training did not prepare me for the insults I got from so-called musicians.

I remember asking a girl with a strange package on her back, "What grade are you on your instrument?" Her reply put me to shame, "Too high for you to be asking." She was a cellist by the way, and I was the humble recorder player. All that week, I had the humiliation of playing percussion. Not that percussion is a bad set of instruments, but in a large orchestra, it might as well have been. I was told I did not count and should simply give up by all the other kids at the camp.

I remember sitting there crying and thinking, 'What am I going to do?' This recorder thing simply isn't going to cut it. Then, I heard it, the sounds of a powerful lyrical bass line. It came out of nowhere with a percussive infectious groove. This was the playing of the Contrabass Saxophone, played by a talented sixteen-year-old who played a saxophone taller than he was. He was my first inspiration, suddenly my tears dried up and I just had to know what that instrument was.

I hurried to the recreation room and asked. I was told it was called the saxophone, and there started my love affair with my instrument, which honestly has never let up.

I remember asking my father to buy me a saxophone. He wanted me to play the French Horn, but after two years of begging, he relented. I started playing the saxophone when I was fourteen, and it was a tough struggle.

Most teachers do not realise that in high school, musicians are not respected. We are the butt of jokes, and we never get the credit for all the work that we put in. It is no different in Zimbabwe. I remember being the only person in my whole school who would practise three times a day to pass examinations. I would practise in the morning for thirty minutes before school, I would practise for an hour at lunchtime at school, and practise for forty-five minutes when I got home.

I remember wanting to write my grade 8, ABRSM examination. My saxophone, which I had of course pimped out with the best mouthpieces, ligature and reeds I could find, was stolen. It even had a custom case that Dad had imported all the way from France. To make matters worse, land reform had just started in

Zimbabwe, and examiners were not coming to Zimbabwe because Zimbabwe was an unsafe country.

I remember not being able to write my grade 8, ABRSM examination in 2001 because of this. Everything was uncertain. I looked to the adults to make things happen; being nineteen at the time, I still trusted them. Nothing happened. When 2002 came round, I still could not write my examination.

I took the initiative and called the Associated Board in London. I explained my situation, and they agreed to transfer the examinations of myself, my two brothers, and sister to South Africa, where I had a family friend who would accommodate us. That was the end of my troubles.

I had to find an accompanist; I found a Japanese lady who I fought with - tooth and nail. We really did not see eye to eye with the repertoire. I remember thinking to myself, something is really wrong when she plays the piano, I don't know where I am, and this doesn't sound anything like the recording. She assured me, she knew what she was doing, but it never sounded right to me.

The night before we - my brother Zikile, who played piano and clarinet, Dumile, French Horn and trumpet, and my sister Lathizile on flute and oboe - were due to go to South Africa our accompanist called to cancel. She said that she had played the pieces for her own teacher, and her teacher Mrs. Wright, said her playing was so bad that she must cancel as we would fail the exam as the accompanist was not up to scratch.

Well, what were we to do? I phoned the exam coordinator and told her that we needed an accompanist and to make it happen by 6 pm the following day when we arrived in Johannesburg for the examination. My saxophone had leaks and was really unstable, as it was a loaner instrument I had borrowed from the local university. I was not giving up as there was just too much at stake.

We arrived in Johannesburg at 4 pm after a sixteen-hour bus

ride. We went to the accompanist's house and had two run-throughs each. It sounded really different and for the first time, since getting the accompanist, I knew I could play, it could happen.

When we were about to leave, Mrs Muterera, our host told the accompanist that she would have to supply transport to get us to the examination tomorrow because she could not as she was expected at work. I remember the accompanist being livid, but after some persuasion, she agreed to take us to the examination.

It was a really cold day in October 2003 when I wrote my Grade 8, ABRSM saxophone exam. My fingers were frozen. I cannot remember how well I played, but I do remember the examiner asking our accompanist to take us home.

After all this, I passed. For me, this is what taking the lead means.

Author Bio:

Thulane Akinjide-Obonyo, is a professional saxophonist and saxophone coach. He specialises in teaching people how to play the saxophone by ear so that they may unlock the true power of jazz and traditional folk music.

https://www.facebook.com/playsaxnow

11

ALWAYS HAVE A DREAM

Sherry St. Germain
United States

I was on TV by the time I was eight months old - on my father's national television music show *Ray St. Germain Country*. I started piano lessons at age two. By age four, I would fall asleep with my yellow Walkman listening to jazz, mostly Bill Evans and Oscar Peterson. I was obsessed. Little did I know I would travel the world, play a flying piano and become a multi-instrumentalist and music producer. From a very young age, my life had an itinerary. I was chosen to study music at the Gifted Youth Music Program at the University of Manitoba while going to grade school. I loved it so much.

I had performed in bars with my father and his band since I was ten years old. I could be found sneaking into clubs at fourteen with my older brothers for karaoke competitions.

At fifteen, I left home and school to play piano for "Bob's Wild West Show" with my brother DJ and nephew Jeff (who was also known as my other brother). It was a caravan of four to five trucks and horse trailers that traveled southern Manitoba. There was a stunt show with horses, with the band accompanying as they performed. The band would play all night and party till all hours of the morning. We were always playing. Even when we were partying, we were studying music - growing, and learning while having fun.

These were my formative years. We learned and traded multiple riffs to our musical vocabulary. The more riffs we learned, the more vocabulary we had to speak with, and the more musically fluent we became.

I remember going to raves and writing theory patterns down on napkins. The theory lessons my momma taught me were helping me tremendously. I was decoding the craziest live bass house records, all by ear, and writing it numerically on a napkin.

I was really studying at these events while having fun.

It is amazing that the things you think were boring when you're a kid, (practicing scales/theory) turn out to be your greatest gifts and assets.

One day, I opened the yellow pages right onto a page called Precursor Productions. I was sick of telling someone how I wanted things to sound so I decided to take my career into my own hands. That began my obsession with production. I learned how to produce and studied multiple instruments.

I moved to Vancouver to live with my sister Cathy. Her now-husband Mike Reno (Loverboy), hooked me up with EMI. In 2009, my album *Kick out the Lights* was featured in *Billboard Magazine* naming me as Best Upcoming Artist.

I wrote songs for and with people that I never met. I lived in New York, then Philadelphia ,then Miami, Toronto, etc. I lived with Jay-Z`s and N.E.R.D"s keyboard player. He and his wife, Danita, made me feel like family and taught me a lot, including how to play the "Philly-trilly".

This went on for several years until I got a call to join Cirque du Soleil in Las Vegas and perform in the "Viva Elvis" show at the Aria. I sang and played a flying piano from 2009 to 2011. (Yes, that was cool.) I also got to sing a duet with the late great Elvis Presley and released the song on an album.

What I learned there were the most valuable things I've ever learned about hard work. It took endurance, rehearsals, and lots of practice to stay at the top of my game.

I had an accident in the show. I broke my ribs which led to being on pain pills. I developed fibrotic tumors, endometriosis, fibromyalgia, and a permanently dislocated rib. I was dependent on painkillers for chronic pain till 2014. I endured surgeries, pills, therapists, and years filled with nights of agony with zero quality of life.

I was booked for surgery one more time. In the three weeks prior to surgery, I watched documentaries about how a raw vegan diet could cure autoimmune diseases.

Being a sceptic, I approached with caution. I was at my wit's end and beyond exhausted with no one fixing me just putting Band-Aids on the problem. I was willing to try anything.

In three weeks, I went for surgery. Following a pre-surgical scan, the doctor said, "What did you do?" My mother was there, witnessing this with me. We were all shocked that I was completely healed. All of a sudden, I had my life back. I realized that what you eat affects your brain's processing power for studying and learning music. It is even as simple as staying hydrated. My friend Christina told me something that stuck: Diet equals mood.

If you're not healthy you can't do anything.

My connection with music only got better once I respected my body and mind. I had a good run with no problems until a few years later. I fell and smashed my head into the ground with a severe concussion that led to a brain injury.

This happened as I was being taken off of a drug that had

been prescribed by my doctor to help me focus my then ADHD. I had an insane schedule of touring, performing, and staying up all night creating film pitches.

I had over 100 placements in TV and film. It was such a rush to play the lottery and win one of these placements. I would be given twenty-four hours to finish something, completely mastered and ready for release. Ultimately, the heavy schedule took its toll - and I prayed.

The universe sent me a healer that told me about the 528hz healing frequency that repairs broken DNA. I would use it with headphones, rocking back and forth, and could feel it actually repairing my brain. The power of frequency changed my life.

I am so grateful my career has allowed me to continue producing and performing at such venues as Tomorrowland in Belgium and Poland with Steve Aoki; Tmobile Arena in Las Vegas, New York's Madison Square Garden, and all the greatest festival shows an artist could only dream of.

My passion led me to my heart and soul project "Akylla" - as producer/singer/writer. Follow your passion - Dream Big. As my Granny Rose would say... "Always Have a Dream".

Author Bio:

Sherry St. Germain is a classically trained multi-instrumentalist, producer, and prodigy singer/songwriter. She works closely with Ableton and is sponsored by Roland. Sherry's unforgettable performances showcase her multiple genre productions. Sherry's Akylla project brings another layer to the stage with her band, performing jaw-dropping live electronic music.

https://www.akylla.com/

12

60 YEARS OF WORLDWIDE CONCERTIZING – A WAY OF LIFE

Rami Bar-Niv
Israel & USA

I was born into music, and it became both what I do and who I am.

I did pretty well with my composing, song writing, teaching, and creating a course. I wrote about it in two previous books of the *Power of Why* series. I'll pass on singing – you do not want to hear me sing.

In recent years, I have also been the sole administrator of six internet piano/music groups totaling about 30,000 members. However, my main career was performing as a concert pianist. I traveled extensively concertizing all over the world. I was a soloist with orchestras, a recording artist with Columbia Records and other labels, I recorded for radio and television stations worldwide, and I was in demand as a chamber-music pianist. I performed for Leonard Bernstein, Arthur Rubinstein,

Isaac Stern, and various other musicians of the Golden Era. I won many scholarships, prizes, and grants.

In 1982, I made history by being the first and only Israeli artist to perform in Egypt following the Begin/Sadat Peace Treaty. In 1989, the Israeli government gave me the annual "Best Performer Award". I was quite a successful pioneer on the internet in its early days and was often at the top of the charts in music sites such as MP3.com, where I had millions of listeners. My current YouTube channel 'barniv' hosts over 100 of my videos. The Foreign Ministry sent me to give concerts in many countries, representing Israel as a goodwill ambassador.

I owe it all to my parents: the education and support they gave me, teaching me that there are no shortcuts but only persistent hard work, and encouraging me to go get it and keep on carrying the torch.

In 1936, at age eighteen, Genia Rechnitz came by herself from Poland to study math at the Hebrew University in Jerusalem and then changed to learning music in Tel Aviv. In 1939, nineteen-year-old Aharon Branover came from Romania on an illegal boat, disembarking in the middle of the night to hide from the British-Mandate soldiers and police. The story of my father's boat trip that was supposed to be three weeks and lasted three months with no food, no drinking water, no medications, and many illnesses, can fill a whole book by itself.

My parents met at the Conservatory of Music in Tel Aviv at the beginning of WWII. Music was their matchmaker. My mother played the piano, and my father played the violin. They started playing café gigs together on weekends, fell in love, and got married. My father's parents, Gitle Shkolnik and Moshe Branover, perished in the Holocaust. My mother's mother, Rachel Lejzerowicz, died as a result of an explosion in the Nazi ammunition plant at the slave-labor camp of Skarżysko-Kamienna. My mother's father, Bernard Rechnitz, and his son, Moishe (the brother of my mother) survived the hell of the

Holocaust by pretending to be dead at a mass shooting of Jews who first dug their own graves.

I was born in Tel Aviv in 1945 – the year WWII ended. It feels like I stemmed from the Holocaust. Despite the sufferings of my parents and their families, despite air-strike bombs on Tel Aviv, and despite various wars that happened when I grew up, I had a very happy childhood. At age two, as my parents told me, I recognized symphonies, concertos, operas, and their composers. My mother started giving me piano lessons at age five, but not before my older brother, Yair, had one day of piano and quit, proclaiming that piano was for girls.

My parents took me to concerts, musical movies, operas, and ballet performances. My mother used to say that she taught me piano so I would be successful with girls. She used to put the only clock we had in the house on the piano and close the door behind her as she left the room so I would practice for half an hour. Every day during my practice, I would move the clock five minutes ahead (didn't want it to be too obvious) so I'd practice for only twenty-five minutes. My parents never understood why that fine clock was five-minutes fast every evening when they heard the 9 p.m. news on the radio.

As a young student I attended many concerts, mainly at the Mann Auditorium in Tel-Aviv, where I would sneak in, like I did in later years (being a poor student) at Carnegie Hall. I also accompanied and played chamber music a lot.

At age eighteen, I entered the Academy of Music in Tel-Aviv. My piano teacher was Karol Klein, a very modest piano virtuoso who immigrated to Israel from Poland. He was a student of Ignaz Friedman and Isidor Philipp, a lawyer and head of a music conservatory in Poland, before immigrating to Israel. I finished the Academy in two years instead of four. Then at age twenty, I did an extra year instead of two for my Artist Diploma.

In September 1966, I went to the USA upon the invitation of

Nadia Reisenberg for whom I had played in a master class in Jerusalem. She was teaching at Mannes College of Music that offered me a scholarship. After graduating from Mannes College of Music in New York, I embarked on a concert career. Giving a concert and preparing for one are sacred to me. I have a near-religious routine of practicing, sleeping, eating, bathing, and warming up on concert days. However, traveling the world for concerts has hardly ever been smooth. Storms strike, flights are delayed or canceled, and luggage often doesn't arrive with me. With all that and my personal life's turbulence and tragedies, I had my hands full yet never gave up.

There were cases where I arrived on the concert stage directly from the airport. I performed as a soloist with the orchestra on the same day we had a stillborn child. I was on a concert tour in the Midwest when our first son was born back East.

I was on tour in Australia when back home, my wife, Andi, miscarried for the third time in a row. I was giving a concert after spending the whole night at the hospital next to my wife who gave birth to our daughter, Sheli, in the morning. A week after the sudden death from the flu of our fifteen-year-old son, Shai, I gave a concert. The next day, Andi and our younger son, Tal, joined me going on a two-month concert tour of the USA.

I don't know if I captured the lead as a musician, but music certainly captured the lead in my life.

Author Bio:

Rami Bar-Niv, international pianist, composer, author, teacher. Born: Tel-Aviv, 1945. Graduated: Rubin Academy of Music, NYC's Mannes College of Music. Founded "Rami's Rhapsody Piano Camp". Authored "The Art of Piano fingering", "Blood, Sweat, and Tours".

http://www.ybarniv.com/rami

13

OUT FRONT

Frances Balodis
Canada

I n the Lead or Out Front. You are right.

Music for Young Children (MYC) was written at just the right time – in 1980. Prior to that time, programs for young children were scarce and not validated. Early childhood research flourished at that time, so parents and teachers were more willing to turn an eye to MYC.

The incorporation of learning styles into MYC made it easily accessible to young children and their parents. Since a parent attends classes with their child, they could better understand how their child learns – and therefore be more accepting of the playfulness and multi-learning styles incorporated into this music program.

The approach in MYC is to have the challenges be "easy, more difficult, difficult, and then easy." This encourages the child to become involved and encouraged and then after the difficult steps, to have a "let down" from that stress by having something easy which the child can master. This keeps MYC students "in the lead".

Ensembles, theory, keyboard, listening, singing, warm-ups and composition forms a multi-focus which is not only piano. It is not *piano* for young children. It is *music* for young children. When MYC was written, print was the best way to advertise. This was before computers, cell phones, and much of the social media we have today. The community newspapers were the ideal place to advertise for teachers and students, so it grew quickly as word spread quickly and efficiently. MYC is an ideal career for women and men at home with a family. This provides an opportunity for a job for families who need another income. It can be full-time or part-time offering flexibility. The quality and uniformity (from one teacher to another) of MYC is important. Coordinators review the class presentation and content. This is a time-consuming and costly endeavor – but, oh so necessary. Families move and can transfer from one teacher to another knowing the consistency and quality of the program will be there. The children of the originator of the curriculum of MYC were three and five years of age. This kept the originator on her toes and ever-in-touch with young children's attention spans and interests. Hence, the playfulness of Fireman Fred and the Dreadful Dancing Dinosaur.

There were musical parents and MYC teachers that contributed valuable material to MYC. This enriched the program – so, it wasn't just from one perspective. All contributions were not accepted, but all were reviewed, and valuable information and ideas were accepted and included into the curriculum. The curriculum, therefore, includes the best ideas of over one thousand teachers. Each contributor feels recognized and rewarded. Something that is important for students continuing their musical training after MYC is that the graduating level of MYC is a recognized Conservatory standard. So, a student who is an MYC graduate has completed their grade one piano – in Royal Conservatory of Music, Conservatory Canada or ABRSM (Associated Board of Royal Schools of Music). This is important – as the next teacher knows where to place that student and doesn't spend needless time backtracking. The annual composition festival is a unique feature of MYC. Every March ,thousands of compositions from children as young as three years (Sunshine I) up to students in Moonbeams III (could be eight, nine, and ten) and also adults (from Music Your Best Choice) are sent to MYC's head office for review by a panel of reviewers. This is a huge and exciting task. The compositions come from around the world and are truly outstanding. This is a unique opportunity for the students – both to enter the world of composing and to have a place to submit some of their creative ideas.

In association with the composition festival there is also a competition for children to submit art for the composition sticker. Every child who submits a composition receives a large, beautiful, customized sticker recognizing their accomplishment. The number of students that a teacher has taught is recognized by a "pin" showing the total number of students he/she has taught (accumulating over the years). This helps the teacher feel recognized for his/her efforts. This helps with motivation, keeps the teacher wearing the student number pin and keeps the out-front feeling. The group size can be as few as three students and as many as six students (and parents). This allows for flexibility in planning classes. It certainly helps teachers make flexible times for teaching.

Many MYC teachers submit their students to festivals – sometimes in rhythm ensemble classes, sometimes in piano solo classes. The students are excited by these opportunities – and perform well. They are proud of what they have accomplished. In these changeable times, many recitals are on Zoom. This allows grandparents and other family members from around the world to join in – proudly watching their offspring's success with everyone feeling good about MYC being out front.

The friendships and camaraderie that are felt among the MYC teachers really gives everyone a boost. This helps keep MYC be out front in the teachers' minds. These relationships last a long time – forty years in some cases and twenty-five years in many cases – and long after the teacher has retired. These relationships keep MYC front and centre forever.

The MYC owners (David and Olivia Riddell) plan bi-annual meetings for all MYC teachers. These meetings are inspirational and motivational. David and Olivia really care about the teachers, as do all the staff at MYC head office.

Do you feel the Out Front in The Lead number one position of MYC? When the choirs, orchestras, school music classes are asked, "Who is an MYC grad?" those students happily relate to their time in this superlative program. Yes, MYC is in The Lead.

Author Bio:

Frances Mae Balodis MEd., ARCT, LCCM (H), LCNCM (H) RMT, MYCC is founder (in 1980) of Music for Young Children and cofounder of CLU, certified NLP and Accredited DISC Training provider and MYC Curriculum Creator. Frances is the Director of The Muskoka Men of Song.

https://myc.com

14

PRACTICE MAKES PERFECT

Laurent Boukobza
France

Practice makes perfect. Is this true? Can it really be true? Let's start with the word *perfect*. Over my forty-five years of piano, I can only conclude that this word is at best, an illusion created by our own minds. Perfection is limited to represent only what one defines as perfect. The problem is that in order to achieve this perfection, standards have to be so low that anyone can ace them. So, can this mentality that everyone should be able to succeed be associated with practicing piano, music, and the arts in general? The answer is a resounding no. Practicing develops skills, one's ability to master his or her craft, but perfection? It is and will always remain, stubbornly, only a concept.

So, specifically, why is it that we can never reach this ideal? Simply put, every time perfection comes along, it brings two friends: expectations and demands. Said differently, I realized that once I could excel in a specific aspect of my instrument, it opened a door to what I could do better. Then, this new door opened another, which opened another, and at some point, it became clear that this journey of discovery would continue forever as my demands and expectations can only aim higher and higher. This learning process is precisely why perfection can't exist. Philosophically speaking, this is the same passage one experiences in every aspect of life. One could never claim a *perfect* education, relationship or family.

Let me share one of my first ah-ha moments. When I was a student at the Paris Conservatory, I attended the concert of a very famous pianist and one of my idols. Part of the program was the twelve Chopin Etudes Op.10, which was among the repertoire I was working on at the time, so I was expecting perfection technically and musically. I was ready to learn from the best. I did learn; however, the lesson was quite different from what I had imagined. The concert began, and despite many technical mistakes, I was instantly pulled in by the depth of the music. I felt as if Chopin himself was speaking to me. The pianist spoke the true language of music, and forever changed my perspective. I realized that the pursuit of perfection extends so much further than technical mastery. My idol understood a level of perfection that I had not yet discovered. That concert opened a new door for me: I was made aware of how much can be found behind the notes. And once we cross the threshold of a new door, we can never go back to our old perceptions as we will forever see the world through new glasses.

Each door opens another world of wonders that could not have been unlocked unless the previous has been mastered. Knowing that we are constantly on the brink of infinite discovery is an incredibly exciting realization that keeps me on the highest of highs all the time.

And this brings me to my next point. Once one discovers the endless number of doors that lies ahead, it becomes apparent that another quality is necessary to continue, modesty. When we realize that the road ahead will never end, we undoubtedly ask ourselves, "How many doors have I gone through so far?" Although we might not ever have a definite answer to this question, the ability to ask for the help and perceptions of others is essential to continue on this journey.

A few years ago, I was lucky enough to speak with Martha Argerich after one of her concerts. She began by thanking me for coming to the concert and by asking if I was a pianist. The conversation continued, "How did you like the concert? The Prokofiev is actually quite difficult..."

I replied, "It was magnificent, and that doesn't surprise me about the Prokofiev."

She looked at me with worried eyes, "You mean you could hear that it was difficult? That means I have to work harder..."

Martha Argerich genuinely demonstrated how modest she is in her willingness to listen to outside perspectives and comments. It is safe to say that if we stop being open to those around us, we may simply stop improving. From the highest-level musicians to the audience members who might have just attended their first concert, everyone may have something to teach us, and it is our choice to have the humility to listen.

Albert Einstein left us with this wisdom: "The more I learn, the more I realize how much I don't know." So instead of focusing on perfection, let's focus on expectations, demands, and improvements. Let's keep a humble approach, take our time, and remain open to this beautiful, endless, door-filled journey — ready to say yes to each wonder and challenge, treating each of these moments as an opportunity to learn.

On my end, I created a YouTube channel where I love to share and educate people who enjoy music and piano. I explain the texts, history, and give musical explanations of all thirty-two of Beethoven's Piano Sonatas, one movement at a time. My hope is to give the listener an idea of what it truly means to expand one's interpretation, which eventually might lead to that ah-ha moment when one first experiences what is behind the notes.

Am I doing this job perfectly? Probably not.

Author Bio:

A Parisian native, Laurent Boukobza is a prize winner of many international competitions, a concert pianist in the process of recording the complete cycle of all 32 Beethoven Piano Sonatas. Laurent tours the world regularly.

https://www.youtube.
com/c/LaurentBoukobzaPianistandTeacher

15

BROTHERS IN MUSIC

Ray St. Germain
Canada

I t is a musician's code that when you play with someone in a
band you develop a connection that is unexplainable. It is a
musical conversation that needs no words. The respect and
mutual admiration for the talent, dedication, and the connection of synergy between "brothers in music" is like no other.

But sometimes brothers in music are much more than you ever
imagined.

As a young boy at age fourteen, I joined a country band "The
Rhythm Ranch Boys" and was hired to play accordion and sing.
When I started singing Elvis songs and rock & roll, the crowd
went crazy. Roy, the band leader, told me I would probably

hurt myself jumping and shaking all over the stage with an accordion - after all, Elvis played guitar. So, he offered to teach me, and I happily accepted. By the age of sixteen, I had developed quite a following and became known as "Winnipeg's Elvis Presley".

Traveling through town came the country music legends show "Hal Lone Pine and Betty Cody" together with their son, the late great jazz guitarist Lenny Breau (known as the wizard on the guitar - and well respected by Chet Atkins). They came from Bangor, Maine and were big stars in the country music scene. They invited me to join their traveling show, and Lenny and I became like brothers.

In addition to traveling shows, they also had a regular CKY radio show, and it was exciting to be part of the experience. I showed up at the CKY radio studios with my new Martin D18 Guitar, ran over some Elvis songs, and got ready to record live to tape. While in Winnipeg, Lenny met my family, including my sister Val. They fell in love, got married - and Lenny truly became my brother-in-law rather than just my brother in music.

Home on the road consisted of country hotels and playing pool at the pool hall after the gig. One night we lost track of time and were late arriving at the CKY studios where Pine was waiting for us with his white stretch Cadillac to drive to the next show out of town. Pine waited till we got there and fired us on the spot. I learned another lesson in show business. And to this day, I'm always early for a gig.

My first television appearance was a cross-Canada singing competition called Talent Caravan on CBC. It was the beginning of a new era that took black and white TV to color television. This was the start of a lifelong television career that featured a big band in the *Like Young Show*. Next, I hosted *Music*

Hop Hootenanny from Winnipeg (with my "brother in music" Lenny Breau on guitar), while Alex Trebeck (yes that *Jeopardy* Alex Trebeck) hosted the show from Toronto.

Another TV show I hosted was *My King of Country*, where I enjoyed working with a rhythm guitar player named Brian Whyte. He was another "brother in music" - talented, respected, and one heck of a musician. People used to ask me if Brian was my brother because we looked alike. Brian and I had become good friends while working on the TV show together.

He had confided in me how he had been raised to believe his grandparents were his mom and dad and his birth mother was his sister. He started searching for his father as soon as he found out the truth. After what seemed like forever, Brian managed to get the files opened up for him, and he discovered his dad's name was Simon Adrien St. Germain from St. Vital. Hey - that's MY dad's name. It was 1977; I was thirty-seven and he was forty-one.

I was playing at the Ramada Inn in Winnipeg when he and his wife came in and waited until a break in the show to tell me that we in fact were brothers. I was stunned. We embraced and cried. Here was a good friend who had told me many times about wanting to find his father when we were on the road playing shows. I always hoped his father was still alive and wished he could connect with him.

Brian's mother had been my dad's girlfriend and when she got pregnant, her parents sent her away to have the baby. When she returned with baby Brian, he was raised to believe his grandparents were his mom and dad and his birth mother was his sister. This was four years before my dad met my mom.

I kept staring at him all through the gig and could see my father's features. We went back to the house after the gig, and I introduced my newfound brother to my wife, Glory.

The next day, I went to my parents' house to break the news. But how? I took my mom shopping and said to her in the car,

"Last night there was a woman in the lounge who said she knew dad before you did. I think her name was Leslie (Brian's mom)." My mom said, "You found Brian." I nearly drove off the road. I asked her to explain, and she did. Mom knew that dad had fathered a child four years before they were married but thought they had moved away with Brian, and they would never be in contact with him anymore, so they never told my siblings and me. It was just a few days before Father's Day that my dad got to meet Brian for the first time. It was a special bonding moment as another "brother in music" had come into the fold.

My greatest joy has not only been recording albums, hosting over 500 national television shows, twenty plus years of radio including *The Metis Hour X 2*, performing in multiple countries, receiving prestigious awards including the Aboriginal Order of Canada, and being inducted into the Canadian Country Music Hall of Fame, but simply, being part of the world of musicians - my "brothers in music" who led me to perform in a gospel quartet called "Brothers on a Journey".

I have been blessed to have a beautiful family, who have all performed on stage and on television shows with me numerous times. My latest album is entitled *Life Ain't Hard* because when you've got your family and your "brothers in music" to share your passion with - then life ain't hard.

Author Bio:

Ray St. Germain is a singer/songwriter, recording artist, television host & producer. He has received the Lifetime Achievement Award, Order of Manitoba, Queen Elizabeth II Diamond Jubilee, Aboriginal Order of Canada and is in the Canadian Country Music Hall of Fame.

https://www.facebook.com/ray.s.germain

16

THE SECRET LAND

Swetha Salveps
India

"Life isn't complete without Music,
Day isn't fulfilled without Music,
Every millisecond of existence,
Music what Exists"

It was a cloudy evening with thunder rain which scared me a lot and I hid myself with all the blankets. It happens every time when I hear that sound. Scary, isn't it? But that changed later. My papa came, and he asked me to enjoy and listen to the sound of thunder and drops of heavy rain. I did, and the next day, he bought me a small keyboard and asked me to enjoy the sound of different keys. I just stared at him with lots of confusion and wonder in my mind, "What was he really trying to say?"

The very next day something interesting happened; he left

me in the music class. It all happened when I was eight, not too young by the way, hahaha. I enjoyed the moment, but I was taught by spoon feeding when learning the piano. I was not taught by a professional musician to build a strong base; it was like you are reading the words without any knowledge of the alphabet.

The days were passing, and I was waiting nearly two years to get a perfect mentor. I made my mommy find me a perfect mentor to guide me. Throughout those two years I nagged her every morning, which made her lose weight up to 2 kg. She thanked me later, but that's another story.

I travelled the journey with music and after two years, I was perfect in the alphabets of music. I started to play the keys and experience the sound - whatever I heard and wherever I heard it.

I am grateful to thunder which knocked me into my way of music. Feverish night dreams made me realize how music should be taught with all the joy and fun that I missed during my childhood. This is how it should be taught to all the kids out there who are passionate to learn in this century. The art should reach to every nook and corner of the world.

Every time I took a family trip or function all I could hear was music and composing different tunes which made me calm, patient, and happy along with all the other stuff that I did.

However, I remember my mommy dragging me from one of the events where I stood for a long time losing myself in the drum sound and wishing I could play there.

That day, she decided to get a piano for me. It was an ah-ah moment in my life. And I went a little higher to learn more about music, and I also got a violin to play. I experienced different sounds of instruments whenever I got a chance. I started to imagine all the instruments as human beings and shared all my stuff in my mind through music, where it also cooperated calmly and didn't yell back at me.

Showing "I am yours and you are my command" is what I hear whenever I touch any instrument.

One fine day, my mom was making sweet milk for me, and she asked me to check the status of the milk that was kept on the stove. Unfortunately, I started noticing the sound of bubbles on the surface of the milk and left the status of boiling the milk unnoticed until it poured all the way from the vessel and touched the stove. I got a nice scary scolding from my mom, which I will never forget. But I experienced the joy of sound from the milk while it was bubbling.

Gradually, I got a chance to participate in my school cultural teams which boosted my confidence to the next level. The applause music that I heard from the audience and the congratulations tune that I heard from the sweet voice of human beings made me do more of what I really love.

Some of the people were mocking me, but my parents said, "Do what makes you happy and think about the people who like your performance." Those sweet words gave me the fire to succeed more and more. I spent hours and hours in music without checking the clock, which led me to where and what I wanted. It gave me a strong, pleasant feeling to entertain and teach everyone, and I decided to take a step to help others find the joy of performing music which was so lacking in my early life. It made me realize you can do anything and everything on your own when at one point, I was teaching myself.

Perhaps, I couldn't remember how much weight my mommy lost before she got me a lovely piano and accepted what I loved to do. All credit goes to the thunder and my papa who knocked on my door and helped me realize the magic of music that turned my life upside down at a very early stage.

Everyone on earth should experience the magic of playing

music. I believe the whole universe including nature has music to play and that everything is possible with music.

If I raise my hand, you stop. If I wave you forward, you move again.
"Music makes us feel."

When I play instruments by checking the notes on the staff that is preset in front of me, all my treble and bass clef, quaver, and semiquaver notes dance along with the keys that I play. What a magic movement of music that my mind has created. All these magic and sound movements made my path to capture music for my life. All I want you all to do - is just feel the day-to-day sounds.

Author Bio:

Swetha Salveps is a professional educator, piano player and music theory teacher. She is also a composer of various styles on piano and keyboard. Swetha is passionate about teaching kids how to improve their musical skills.

https://www.linkedin.com/in/swetha-salveps

EVERYONE SHOULD SING

Catherine St. Germain
Canada

E veryone should sing.

I didn't want to be a professional singer, I wanted to be an Olympic gymnast. Gymnastics was my life. It got me out of the house.

My mom and dad met in the late 50's singing on a television show in Winnipeg, Manitoba. They got married and within thirteen months they had two daughters; I was the youngest. My mom became a stay-at-home mom and my dad continued to sing and travel.

We moved to Toronto when I was in grade three. My dad

got a TV show where he hosted and sang big band songs. Unfortunately, our time in Toronto was short lived, but the best thing that came out of it was the birth of my baby brother, Ray Jr. We all inherited the ability to carry a tune, and I had a great knack for harmony at which my mom was an expert.

From as far back as I can remember, we were always singing. We sang with my dad at various engagements whenever possible; I was always the back-up singer. We had one of those record players that looked like a suitcase and sang along to our favourites. One album in particular was Frank Zappa's *Overnight Sensation*. My sister Chrystal and I mastered the wacky, jazzy female harmonies on the songs. My dad would come upstairs after a late night at a gig and just look at us and shake his head. I think deep down he appreciated the artistry. Another favourite was Joni Mitchell's *Court and Spark*. I still listen to it to this day and know every note by heart. We listened to all styles of music from The Beach Boys to Led Zeppelin, Jazz to Country, you name it, we loved it all.

By the time I was thirteen, my parents' marriage dissolved, and we moved in with my mom's parents. They had a beautiful console combo record player/radio and my uncle had quite the album collection. What a treat to hear albums on real speakers instead of those little suitcase speakers. I was in grade eight at the time and in the school choir. I actually used to purposely sing flat at choir try out because I wanted to be in art class instead. I always made the choir. My choir teacher formed a small choir with eight of us from the big choir, and we learned the most incredible songs with huge harmonies. She would plunk out our parts on the piano and because we all had a natural ability to hear harmony, there wasn't a need to read music. We performed small concerts at the malls and at school functions. I loved it.

When I was fifteen, my dad was asked to write and produce his own country music television show. He asked my sister and

I to co-star with him. I was reluctant at first because it meant I would have to sing a solo on every show. Eventually, I said, "Yes." That was the turning point for me. I realized quickly how much I loved to sing solo. We welcomed special guests from Nashville, and the show went on for thirteen years.

When I was eighteen, I joined a show band called Rocki Rolletti and went by the name Rita Rigatoni. We did Motown covers and had a TV show for two years. We won the Trans Canada Rock Contest in 1982 and recorded a single with the legendary Bob Ezrin (Pink Floyd, Alice Cooper...) I was determined to become my own person. I moved to the west coast in 1987 and immediately started singing jingles, song demos, and performing in a local pop band. Some of the jingle sessions were pretty daunting. I would arrive and there would be a vocal chart on the music stand. Thankfully, the producer would always play my part on the piano, and I would be able to remember it with one listen. I got pretty good at reading vocal charts, but I always relied on my ear.

In 1990, I entered a contest called Vocal Warz, made it to the finals, and travelled to Toronto. Over 3000 singers had entered, and I was stunned when I won. I got to record with my great friend Daryl Burgess, and he eventually produced my first CD called *Shy Moon*. It received critical acclaim, and I travelled to Nashville several times after that, singing demos for accomplished songwriters. After a few years, I started singing jazz with some amazing musicians and realized I didn't have to choose one style. Record companies and managers were always confused as to where I fit in and to be honest that was fine by me. I didn't want to be labeled. I have travelled the world and shared the stage with incredible world-renowned artists. Not to brag, but can you say, David Foster, Natalie Cole, Paul Rodgers, Bryan Adams, Ray Charles...etc.

I am so grateful that I have been able to share my experience and have mentored, managed, and steered many young artists on their own journeys. Success to me has always been to be able to sing what I want, when I want, and where I want. I have had an incredible career. There have been struggles, but the highs always outweighed the lows. Singing makes me happy. Have you ever heard someone say, "I can't sing."? I always say, "Yes you can." Everyone can sing. Whether or not anyone would enjoy hearing you sing is not important. Singing is a release, and everyone needs a release every now and then, so SING. It's good for your body and soul.

Author Bio:

Catherine St. Germain is an accomplished vocalist, recording artist, television performer with over forty years' experience in the music industry.

https://www.facebook.com/catherine.stgermain.33/

WITH A VOICE AS BIG AS THE SEA

Shirley Wang
Taiwan - United States

I've always loved the Christmas song, "Do You Hear What I Hear?" And a voice as big as the sea told the story that brought goodness and light into the world. This song's direct, simple, childlike quality brings me back to my beginning. For those who are wondering (which is probably everyone who is reading this), my name is Shirley Wang. I am an opera singer, public speaker, and podcast host.

My experience to move people with my voice started at a very young age. The first time I was formally on stage was to deliver a patriotic speech when I was a tiny little three-year-old. The event organizers chose me because I was cute, had a clear voice, an expressive way of speaking, and important politically influential grandparents.

At that age, I didn't understand what it meant to be in the spotlight. All I knew was I had a job to do, and I wanted so badly to do it well. I wanted to make sure everyone understood what my speech was. To this day, I still can recall how emotional the adults were after I finished. While I am not sure, I would want to involve a three-year-old with such propaganda, personally, this was a defining experience that showed me the influence and power of being in front of an audience.

Even as a child, I had a need to express myself. It was imperative to me to make sure the listeners understood the meaning and purpose of my presentation. I still remember my grandmother helping me memorize the speech by going over it while giving me my daily bath. Talk about being vulnerable and naked with your words.

But how did I go from a three-year-old child public speaker to an opera singer?

When I was fifteen years old, I immigrated from Taiwan to the US with my family. Well, the lack of ability to speak English put an end to my public speaking days, at least temporarily. However, I discovered I had a singing voice "as big as the sea". With that, the incredible world of classical vocal literature was introduced to me. I fell in love with it hard and fast.

I could not believe I had the privilege to communicate through my voice with this new means of expression. And the music, it was simply sublime. As it is expressed in Franz Schubert's "An die Musik."

"O blessed art, how often in dark hours,
    When the savage ring of life tightens round me,
    Have you kindled warm love in my heart,
    Have transported me to a better world."

I became obsessed. The powerful emotions, extreme passion, and the tremendous commitment it demands from the singer just kept drawing me deeper and deeper into the vortex. Operatic singing is a complete mind-body-spirit experience. Being on stage, it just became so much more magnified. The contradiction lies in being kept under a potent spell while feeling so wholly liberated and free. I often describe it as running to the edge of the cliff full speed, then leaping off. Instead of falling, you fly. "Vola, vola." As the Italians say. It is a complete departure from the reality of life. It is total exhilaration. It is what I will do for life.

First came the studies, then came the auditions.

Auditions can be nerve-racking. You have to sing to a small poker-faced audience who will decide your fate. However, the fact that I never had much stage fright helped tremendously. I believe it is because I don't see myself as someone in the spotlight. Instead, I see it as my job to do the best I can. And the job is to express, communicate, and move my audience. Whether it is one or two people in an audition or thousands in a concert hall, this commitment to express is how I captured many of my leads.

One of the most pivoting auditions I did was with a Chinese touring orchestra. I was offered an open-ended contract as their featured soloist. The first stop was the Lincoln Center then the Kennedy Center; the list went on. But the story would not turn out as expected. I turned down the offer. The concert programming was full of political propaganda, and I was not three anymore. It was a difficult decision that required a lot of soul searching. I had to truly ponder: "Why do I do what I do?"

After much consideration, I decided to stop auditioning and

took on complete creative ownership for my artistic expressions. I took over booking concerts and created multimedia presentations focusing on messages that mattered to me: with "a voice as big as the sea" to bring goodness and light to my audience. I performed thirty plus concerts every year. It was exhausting but truly meaningful for me. This is what I wanted to do. I was in my element.

Then 2020 hit. I had to bring my outside voice inside.

With isolation and cancellation of live performances, connections of the minds became truly important. So, like the rest of the world, I started spending more time on social media. I noticed so many of my real-life friends and colleagues had been reduced to "Facebook Friends" over time. To remedy this, I decided to start a conversation series on Instagram: "Tuesday Conversation with Friends" to reconnect and share when the world was so displaced and disconnected. Then it grew into a podcast on YouTube and other major podcast platforms. The guest list expanded from my personal friends to artists from around the world. I love sharing their stories, their hearts, and their art. As the concerts return, the connections remain. It is time for the next chapter with my voice as a singer, speaker, and podcast host, along with my new and old friends.

PS. I still enjoy memorizing my music in the bathtub. Some things never change.

Author Bio:

Shirley Wang, operatic soprano, public speaker, podcast host, and international bestselling author. She has performed across the U.S., including Carnegie Hall. Podcast: Tuesday Conversation with Friends features those who make the world more colorful.

https://linktr.ee/ShirleyWang

OUR VILLAGE MUSICIAN ON TV

Edy Rapika Panjaitan
Indonesia

Our village musician has finally appeared on the largest commercial TV show as a part of a team of adjudicators.

I am living in the quarter note ages, a period where I have found many personal challenges against a backdrop of tragedy, where people strive to survive against an overwhelming pandemic. However, I believe this is truly a moment for opportunity, one where I should explore and discover a new chapter of life as a musician who captured the lead. Some people believe that young musicians are tempted by many aspects along their musical journey. To become a leading musician is not as easy as many people think. I'm saying that capturing the lead is not simply having millions of followers or fans but rather becoming someone who can contribute and spread valuable assets to their surrounding communities. I recognize that this world belongs to us. We have to chase the world and live in harmony with this community.

At present, I write articles while sitting inside the National Library in Jakarta, which is the capital of Indonesia. Even during this, my first visit to this gigantic library, I am filled with inspiration. It is often said that books are the windows to the world, a window where you can travel to every corner of the globe, all at your fingertips. I believe so too, and that this *Power of Why* project has inspired thousands of people around the world. It continuously motivates me and ultimately inspires readers through these unique and individual stories by global authors

My gratitude is abundant. I can only express my sincerest thanks to every supportive and generous person surrounding me, including family, friends, colleagues, partners, parents, and students. I believe these people are who God delivered to encourage me along my path. It is simply by God's love, mercy, grace, and favor that they are in my life. Sharing is important to support what is part of an intimate and hopefully inspirational story.

It was an honor to be invited to be part of a national and international jury of a prestigious competition, and I was over the moon. This was the *Got Talent* competition held by the Indonesian Students' Association in The People's Republic of China and the international singing competition organized by Overseas Indonesian Students' Association Alliance.

Furthermore, there was a song writing competition directed by the Ministry of Higher Education, Culture, and Technology in Indonesia. These precious experiences enabled me to achieve an even more successful career as well as being a foremost musician. Becoming a part of a panel was a privilege, and I'm proud that my credibility was finally recognized by the committee. I could not have previously imagined that I could ever be part of this position. I am certain, to become a leading role model, we need surveillance, innovation, and dedication. As a member of a jury, our task is not only to judge but, rather, to educate, inspire, and guide the participants to be ready for their competition. I had a wonderful experience, firstly during the international singing competition, which was supported by the largest commercial TV station in Indonesia, RCTI plus. It was such an amazing journey, and my first time appearing on a television show, *What a Great Record*. My dreams have come true. I am very happy to have been invited to be on a talent show on TV and am so fortunate to be in this position..

The story doesn't end there. Becoming part of the national jury of a song writing competition followed. The jury members and I started to arrange a guidebook for this competition, including a regional selection all the way to the final round. What a great chance. I learned earnestly how to deal with crucial issues, especially problem solving, giving insights, debating, and reviewing the previous events – this included proposed rejuvenation, as this was a new category in the festival.

Eventually, after several meetings, the chairman agreed on the finalist. On the day of the competition, the panel finally made their decision for the winner, and they really found this difficult – there were so many talented high school students who were able to compose such wonderful music. This was an inspirational experience. It really moved my heart, and I teared up listening to their music.

The juries were really at a loss as to who should become the finalist as each of us also had our own choice. But as a jury, we had to give marks fairly, based on each individual's capabilities, their potential, and many other aspects including, uniqueness and originality. After we had decided, we came up with a final rank. This was fascinating. In addition, when judging the incredible talent of Indonesian students overseas, it really did show to me the wealth of talent that my country has. I was so inspired.

I felt that I also grew during that time, learning and educating simultaneously. This confirmed to me one more issue - stop judging talent by comparison. Competitions are the right place where you can train and experience all your life skills and meet new friends and mentors to help you develop those skills. It reminded me how I reconciled with a competition, and sometimes you win but also sometimes you lose, but I kept on daring to dream. As a member of the jury, I had tried to deliver motivational speeches and offer insights, and I hope these words helped participants to keep on moving forward and seize every opportunity that there is to make music.

There are thousands of millennial musicians who are capturing the lead now, and you should consider doing so too. Many senior musicians are also inspired and share their heritage, legacy, and masterworks. I must realize that the potential is inside me, and you should recognize this too and build up your own power. I strongly believe that to become a leading musician you have to be an optimist, try to create your own revolution, and focus on making an impact.

Another aspect of these forefront musicians are their moments of doubt and despair. The market is huge, and competitors grow day by day. I urge you to create something new and innovate your ideas to make a change. As a young musician you must decide from now on, even though you may have failed in some respects, you still must wake up and take action.

As long as music speaks, you will find a way to follow your own path. Think to yourselves: Where are you now? What has been done, and what needs to be done?

Are you planning or pursuing your music study? Becoming a composer? Dreaming to be a concert pianist? Maybe the most sought-after piano teacher? A famous musician and artist? List your dreams and strive to attain them – always have hope. These difficult paths you tread are all part of the learning process but work hard because discipline is the most valuable secret key.

Chase your dreams; capture the lead NOW.

Author Bio:

Edy Rapika Panjaitan is the founder of Panda Piano Course, Indonesian pianist, music educator, composer, international best-selling author and adjudicator.

http://pandapianocourse.com

RIPPLES IN THE WATER

Julianne Warkentin
Canada

"I alone cannot change the world, but I can cast a stone across the waters to create many ripples." Mother Teresa

I lived near a small rickety bridge when I was a child. It was surrounded by elm trees that reached out their branches to create an enchanting tunnel over a narrow river. I would often stand by the railing, take different sizes of stones, and throw them in the water one by one. I loved watching the unique rippling effect each one had. There was something so calming and hopeful about seeing even one small stone create waves. Nature was teaching me an important life lesson.

We are all leaders in our own way because we all influence others just like the stones cast into the river. Every thought, word, and action impacts everything around us, especially the people on our path. Even if we choose to withdraw, the world experiences a loss from our unused gifts and unique potential. Some of us may be big stones that create an impressive splash yet most of us are smaller stones who presume our *ripples* have little influence. But is that true?

As a little girl, I often gathered neighborhood children to teach them about music or anything else I found interesting. After years of piano lessons, I started teaching lessons myself when I was in high school. My married sister Loraine told me she was expecting her second child and she asked me to temporarily teach her students. Her confidence in me laid a foundation I was able to build my career on. Loraine was also a positive role model to me and an example of diligently pursuing music and teaching and nurturing children. I remember dreamily watching her practice piano at home with her long hair flowing behind her. My big sister was very inspiring.

It didn't take me long to realize I loved being a piano teacher, so I pursued an education in piano performance after graduating high school. I valued the weekly time in my music studio with students exploring the piano and learning what was important to them. I love that private music teachers are unique in this role of consistently spending time alone with a child for many years and therefore becoming a major influence in their life.

I attended my first workshop led by a composer shortly after my own children were born. Canadian piano composer Remi Bouchard presented his creative compositions for young students. I had never met anyone like him before and I thought his career was fascinating. I had composed occasionally for special events like weddings, but his workshop inspired me to pursue publishing with students in mind. It seemed like an impossible dream in the beginning, but I tried to remember he was also a teacher from a small town, just like myself.

Remi lived out the quote by Goethe: "Boldness has genius, power and magic in it." He was a quiet man who courageously lived his dream and led others to do likewise.

It has been rewarding to see some of my students become professional musicians and teachers, but I really appreciate the students who have told me I was a mentor to them and someone who made them feel special. I feel so blessed that many of them have kept in touch with me over the years. It has also been wonderful to guide students to create their own original compositions. For example, my student Andrea composed a reflective, peaceful piano solo entitled "Thoughtful" when she was only fifteen. It is often the first song I play on the piano when doing music therapy at the local hospital's psychiatric ward.

I have also been amazed by students like Gareth who can spontaneously compose whatever he is feeling at the time or Micah, who was an inspiring singer/songwriter even as a young boy. I have watched teenage girls express in music what words could never accomplish. It has been so meaningful to be part of this process. Then there are the compositions about animals. I was not surprised to discover that pets were the greatest source of inspiration for younger children since they often consider their pet to be their best friend. Every "pet song" is as unique as their furry friends. I composed "Peculiar Pets" and "Franny and Friends" with this in mind.

My author friend Terrie was often in charge of church musicals, dramas, and banquets that I was involved in when we lived in the same city. I learned so much through those experiences on many levels. Not only was Terrie a great leader, but she demonstrated how to encourage other artists and musicians so they could continue to blossom in their talents. There were times I felt like she believed in me even when I didn't believe in myself. She encouraged me to focus on the big picture instead of the tunnel vision of perfectionism I struggled with. I have saved many "Dear Jules" encouragement notes she gave to me.

One special day stands out to me in our friendship. We met for coffee and shared struggles and obstacles in our creative and spiritual paths. It meant a lot to me to talk to someone about this part of my life. Although she was successful in many ways, she told me that she had become discouraged in her dream to become a novelist and asked me to pray for wisdom and guidance for her. Later that day, I took some time alone to meditate and pray.

Suddenly, I had a vivid picture in my mind of Terrie seated atop an old-fashioned silver suitcase. It was stuffed full of papers that were obviously trying to get out - the message was clear. Not long after, Terrie Todd released her award-winning debut novel called *The Silver Suitcase* followed by many more fantastic books. I was so very happy for her and admired her talent and hard work so much. Her generous acknowledgement to me in the back of this book was such an honor and life lesson for me. What seemed like a small gesture of friendship on my part made a difference in her life, and she certainly did the same for me.

Never underestimate the power of just being yourself, living your truth, and small acts of kindness. Make your passion into your purpose and others will be inspired to follow your example. The ripples you make in this world matter more than you may ever realize.

Author Bio:

Julianne Warkentin is a creative Canadian Composer, inspiring piano teacher, festival adjudicator, performer and presenter. Her piano solos are published in beginner to advanced levels. She leads composition workshops with students to inspire them to compose.

https://www.instagram.com/julianne.piano/

21

THE MAGICAL HEALING POWER OF
MUSIC

Alyse Korn
USA

L ove of music, movement, and spiritual connection run
through my life and work. Staying true to my passion and
joy for sound, music, and helping others brings me back to my
Why whenever I need a reminder.

I was born into a musical and artistic family in Miami, Flor-
ida, a vibrant city and cultural melting pot, so I met many
unique people and experienced many cultures (Cubans, Puerto
Ricans, Jamaicans, Trinidadians, South Americans and more).
This medley of sights, sounds, languages, and musical styles
were so significant to my musical education.

I was inspired by my family, too. My grandmothers, both
trained classical pianists, were my first teachers. I spent hours
sitting on their laps, watching, and touching the keys. My whole
family was musically and artistically minded. My uncles played
the clarinet and Blues Harp; Dad played American Jazz, British
Rock, and Afro-Caribbean music. Mom listened to American

Folk and painted. I loved to look at the artwork and read the liner notes on my parent's LPs.

As a very active person, I learned to connect the body, mind, and spirit naturally through music, salsa dancing, and other athletic pursuits such as riding horses, swimming, and martial arts. I've always had a desire or passion for learning more and going deeper. Music has always felt like an essential part of connecting to the soul.

As a sensitive soul, it took me a while to find my tribe and a nurturing, creative environment as a child. However, my adult life strengths are the same traits that got me bullied as a child, being different, and unafraid to be an outsider. My sensitivity is my superpower.

I found my niche in a Gifted Student program in Elementary, Middle School, and then the highly creative environment of Dillard Performing Arts High School and the Jazz Band and Orchestra. From then on, I noticed Magical connections forming with mentors, friends, and places. People would come into my life at just the right time, or I would find myself in that right place at the right time. Opportunities found me: a working Big Band, an Indie-Rock Band, and the Dade and Broward Community College Jazz Bands.

Called back to Miami for university, I had all the passion and desire to study, yet I struggled mightily. In the Studio Music and Jazz Department, there were absolutely no women mentors other than the women in the vocal department. I had a very negative experience with some male professors in tenure and their intense Yang energy. There were many moments of crying and feeling like I wasn't good enough and didn't belong. They did everything in their power to push me out. Other male professors suggested that I take up music education rather than Studio Music and Jazz. The attitude was that women should be teachers rather than performers. Maddening.

I stood up for myself and went to see the Dean of the School of Music, a female tuba player. She approved me to work with Ron Miller, the Jazz Composition teacher and a tremendous influence on my path as a Jazz pianist, composer, and performer. He was Yin to my previous teacher's Yang approach to learning. Ron's system of harmony and composition opened up a whole world of creativity and confidence in my abilities as a composer and jazz pianist.

I fell in love with learning, composing, and performing again, graduating with high marks and a joyful, successful senior recital with my family in attendance. My classical piano teacher at the same university, Dr Sackstien, paved the way for me to meet her son-in-law David Roitstien, director of the Jazz Department at CalArts in Valencia, CA, who accepted me into the Master's program and hired me as a Teaching Assistant. I enjoyed community teaching for kids, too. When teaching became a choice rather than expected, I embraced it.

Feeling free and inspired, with an abundance of creativity flowing, I loved my new tribe. I had found my people. There were no grades, only pass or no pass. I was far from my family of origin and learning to stand on my own two feet.

The World Music Program opened up a fierce connection to expressing myself through music, movement, voice, dance, drumming, and collaborating with a community of like-minded artists. David and the committee chose my composition for the 2nd edition of CalArts Jazz CD recorded at Capitol Records, boosting my confidence as a composer, performer and recording artist.

At this point, I fell in love with African Music & Dance, Indonesian Gamelan, and Indian music studies. So, I brought these all together with Jazz and Latin-Jazz piano studies and started teaching and performing in Los Angeles during my CalArts studies.

I was invited to join the Music Teachers Association of California and became an active member and volunteer, a local chair volunteer, and then a state chair volunteer. In addition, I led many student programs and acted as an adjudicator. Another magical connection was with a Suzuki piano method teacher in Orange County, Maxine Casper, who encouraged me to certify in all levels of Suzuki piano and Early Childhood Education music and create an incredibly successful Suzuki teaching and mentoring career.

Alongside teaching, I've performed for Theatre and T.V., countless Jazz, Latin-Jazz, Salsa and Brazilian performances in Los Angeles, nationally and abroad.

I became interested in Sound Healing after an injury during my Doctoral Studies at USC, and this is where music and energy in healing practices started to coalesce for me. So how does this all come together?

The joy I get from seeing a person's talent blossom is matched by seeing someone find clarity in confusion or feeling a weight lift off their shoulders after a Biofield Tuning session or other treatment. The energy I feel coursing through me through music and dance is the healing energy I channel into treatments. Following my heart and intuition has not always been easy, but it's always been worth it. Now I teach people how to follow theirs.

I first started practicing meditation, yoga, Reiki, and other spiritual studies during my teenage years to heal from my parents' divorce and a household that was emotionally unhealthy and unstable. I experienced trauma as a child and as an adult through a controlling and abusive relationship. Like many healers, I started with the need to heal myself, which spurs me to help others heal. I'm now in a happy, healthy, and loving relationship. My exploration in music and spirituality, and the blend that brings to my work, is truly special to me. That's my why.

Author Bio:

Alyse Korn is a musician, sound healer, teacher, and mentor, based in Ojai. I lead students to succeed and thrive at Ojai Suzuki Piano School. I weave music and sound healing together at Alyse Korn Music and Healing with Alyse.

www.alysekornmusic.com

MY MUSIC JOURNEY

Bridget Mwape
Botswana

My music teaching journey started when I was first introduced to music theory in church as a teenager, which was something very new to us. I was fascinated by the fact that one could learn how to read music while singing or playing an instrument which was something I did not know before.

We had a group of volunteers who taught music theory at different after church services and my interest in music theory grew because I did not find it very hard to comprehend what we were learning. I was later appointed to teach in church and travelled across the country in my native country conducting music lessons and exams. Although I play a couple of musical instruments, I was captivated by a deep desire to explain to the students how despite our perception concerning music theory, it can be done. The challenge was to teach students whose first language was not English and therefore we had to explain in our local languages when teaching. This can sometimes be challenging because some terminologies cannot be found in local languages. In the end, it worked out.

I moved to a different country, my present country of residence, and I continued to volunteer as a music teacher in my church which I still do today in my capacity as music coordinator. I was later formally employed at a music academy. It became an opportunity to learn more about music theory, and I keep learning every day,because I found out that there were many things I was yet to learn in order for me to be an effective teacher. This led to a lot of personal study and research and taking graded exams until I took Grade 8 Theory exams and passed. It was an achievement on my part because I had to do most of the work on my own. I was later appointed as the examination coordinator at my place of employment of which one of the job descriptions is to prepare candidates for exams. My determination to help as many students as I could was increased because if I was able to do it, then I could guide them on the music theory journey. The reason why I keep teaching to this day is to see my students understand music theory because it also helps them apply the knowledge when it comes to playing musical instruments.

In June of 2021, I opened a music studio, BridgerTone Music, a private music studio offering lessons in music theory and different musical instruments to students of all ages, from children to adults. Why children? Because along the way, I have come to understand the benefits of music education in children and adults. The aim is to teach students on a one-on-one basis as well as in groups. With the pandemic still looming, it became a challenge to meet physically for classes and then came the idea of holding online classes via Zoom. Due to some technological challenges on this side of the world, the easiest platform to use as an option was Zoom. BridgerTone Music offered a first free music lesson to children less than eight years of age to show that it can be done whether in person or online. The feedback from parents was overwhelming. It has become something that I will continue doing in the long run. A YouTube channel was also recently opened for BridgerTone Music and lessons are uploaded every week. I am just starting out and hope to grow.

The desired outcome I have is to see students read music properly whether when singing or playing an instrument, and I believe this can be achieved through thorough teaching of music theory and application will bring to an end the culture of individuals wanting to play or sing as long as they can produce a sound. Not only that, careers can also be built from learning music which can be a form of income for many.

Author Bio:

My name is Bridget Mwape, a music teacher and director of BridgerTone Music. I am also an accomplished Flutist and a member of the Apostolic Faith Church orchestra. I have a Grade 8 in Music theory and Flute playing and currently studying for LMusTCL.

https://www.linkedin.com/in/bridget-mwape-515022183

23

BREAK THE RULES AND TELL YOUR STORY

M. Elizabeth Garland
USA

"I f your story is better told by breaking the rules, then, by all means, break the rules."

I was never a true rebel. It's kind of embarrassing. I tended to follow the rules, color inside the lines, make the grades, and practice the required hours of piano. I took the lead when expected. Although, I am proud to say that I was compelled to stand up against injustice when I saw it. I was sort of in awe of anyone who truly bucked the system.

My dad was the quintessential rule-breaker. He loved to stand out. Tall, with a bushy silver mustache and a long braid, he dressed in cut-off shorts for meetings in Santa Fe with the governor. He wore sneakers and t-shirts (way before it was cool) to court corporate CEOs. He never stood on ceremony with anyone. If the church sermon ran five minutes late, he simply stood up, looked at the preacher, vigorously tapping his watch, and walked out, my three brothers and I following behind with my mortified mother. My dad had charm enough to get away with bending the rules and speaking his mind - most of the time. Though he made his fair share of enemies and was proud of that, too.

I tried rebelling eventually, after my childhood came to its abrupt end. It was liberating, if maybe a little exhausting. I smoked too many cigarettes and lived a bohemian life for a while, rooming with artists, writers, and musicians of the non-classical variety. It was such a departure from my private school, highly religious upbringing that it came with its own learning curve. It was my attempt at the Paris of Hemmingway, Joyce, and Gertrude Stein.

I found platforms to express myself – painting, bad poetry, and music. My compositions at that time spoke more than I could about the pain and fear and sadness that had been imprinted on my soul by the battery and ensuing suicide of my aunt, the care-taking of my schizophrenic uncle, the rage and depression that lived under the surface of our perfect family. My attempts at art attested to the desire to make it on my own terms somewhere between two worlds in which I didn't really fit: the Arts and the artists.

I was classically primed. My youth was laser focused on success, scholastic achievement, and proving my talent. I knew the rules about succeeding in the arts. A pedigreed artist attends a great school and pursues his or her advanced degrees at a different incredible school. He or she must have a circle of contacts with influence. Don't forget the mentors who make those exacting demands and have all the impressive qualifications. And one simply must debut before one's expiration date...by at least age. (You might skip any one of these qualifications if you had money.)

So, while I realized that nothing other than a career in the arts would satisfy my soul, I also believed I had a pretty slim chance of success. I had only won one state piano competition in high school. Honestly, there wasn't much hope because I didn't go to Juilliard, had never even applied to Berklee, to Oberlin, or NYU. I went to a state school. I taught piano during the day and bartended at night to make ends meet. I could have just accepted my fate teaching piano and writing music that no one would ever hear, but there was always that voice inside, insisting that I push on and break some rules to write my own story.

Every time someone who made it to the top without the proper qualifications came to my attention, I filed it away. Edward Elgar, the English composer, was never formally trained in composition. Einstein had no degree. Walt Disney never graduated high school, yet his vision created an empire. Georgia O'Keefe was in her later years before she attained fame. Barbra Streisand, Rachel Portman, and Hildur Gudnadottir are Oscar winning female composers. I read and still read so many books about never giving up. I became a bit obsessed, but I think you must be passionately driven if you are going to try to break the glass ceiling. We must be, all of us - the dreamers of dreams. What I lacked in true self-confidence, I made up for in bravado and faith.

I prayed to God, to the gods, to the goddess. I made the kind of desperate bargains that artists make. Such as promising I would work harder than I'd ever worked and knock on every door if they would bring the magic. Because I did believe in magic, and I still do. I held tight to the promise that God could make a way where there was no way. And then I worked: composing, applying for everything, learning finale in and out, getting pro-tools certified, studying scores for film and symphony. I then became an award-winning composer.

I found another secret ingredient to the magic: gratitude. Gradually, I stopped focusing on all the things I wasn't. I let myself be enough. I realized that my hometown piano teacher had gifted me with far more than classical music knowledge. She trained me to focus intently, to listen deeply, and to commit. I embraced how wonderful my mom was. She had given me so much love, music lessons, and a love of film, old Hollywood movies with gorgeous full orchestral scores.

I scored my first films. I forgave myself for not following that well-trodden path. The travel on a shoestring budget I did in my twenties had trained me to depend on my own instincts and to communicate non-verbally. The choices I made led me to have two beautiful children, incredible little girls, who make their own magic and who are so committed to the truth of their play. Suddenly, my Why had become transformed from showing everyone I had value to making the world a better place for these creatures to explore. And if I have taken the lead, it's because I love to work at this work.

In the end, I think it is all about perception. What spin do you put on your own existence?

If you believe it is beautiful and magical it becomes so and opportunities begin to arrive. The most amazing people fall onto your path. Right now, I am, oddly, producing a music film. I am a novice again. I get to rehearse in person and record with my ensemble this weekend for the first time since Covid began.

And I have no idea what the journey will look like from here because there really are no rules.

Author Bio:

Elizabeth Garland is an award-winning composer, best-selling author, and speaker residing in New Mexico. She teaches a course on composition and creativity. She is passionate about film scoring, and loves to travel, swim and laugh.

http://www.elizabethgarlandcomposer.com

24

THE JOY OF TEACHING

Raymond Ross
Canada

I am one of many music teachers in the world that helps music flow from one generation to the next. Music is and always has been one of my strongest passions: the playing for fun, the thrill of performing, the rehearsing, and most of all, the flow of emotion from one heart to the next.

Earlier in Life

As a young man, I began to consider my career options. High school was soon coming to a close and the next chapter of my life was beginning. I had done research into my options as a musician and how I might create a career out of the activity that for so many years had been the focus of much of my energy, passion, time, and heart. I concluded that my options were to become a music educator or become a traveling concert pianist/performer.

However, I wanted to have a family one day and so travelling as a musician didn't seem to fit my long-term goals and desires. From what I gathered, teaching was a good option but required a lot of schooling that, at the time, I did not want to pursue. Teaching in the public school system was the most financially attractive, or so I thought. However, I wasn't drawn to the idea of teaching kids music who weren't serious about it, and so that took care of teaching in a public school system. I stopped pursuing this vocation seriously at this point.

Off I went into the world listening to family, friends, media, and the music industry about what the best careers were. I went ahead and was employed in most sectors of the work force only to come away empty-handed and empty-hearted. Fast forward a decade after graduating high school – things were much different at this point. I had attended three years of trade school, two years of university, worked in sales, retail, and human services. I was married to the woman of my dreams, and we were expecting our first baby. I had now started a family and the following question weighed heavily on my mind and heart – "How might I provide well for my family and get up each morning looking forward to my workday?" Up to this point, I had listened to everyone but myself about what I truly wanted to do. I taught private music lessons intermittently throughout the past decade. Teaching privately has always been in the background of my story. I suppose I just couldn't stay away from teaching regardless of my previous conclusions about it.

The Build Up
When I really reflected on teaching privately as a career, I

remembered how I always loved showing friends how to play music on the piano. I always loved entertaining and showing people that with some hard work, dedication, and a genuine desire to improve you could become great at whatever truly makes you happy. Moreover, as I reflected on all of the above, my value in the workforce, the impact my music teacher had on my life, and how I might be able to share my gifts and talents with others, it became crystal clear what I wanted and needed to do. I came to the conclusion that I must do what makes me happy, find a way to provide for my own family while doing it, and make a difference in the lives of others with the gift I've been graciously given. With all of that in mind, I finally gave myself permission to go ahead and begin building my very own music studio.

When I decided to go forward with this, I experienced many emotions. Fear of success prevailed my fear of failure because I knew deep down that this is what I was meant to do and that it would work. In addition, self-doubt and insecurity in both my teaching and my business ownership skills were prevailing thoughts. I often wondered why anyone would want to learn music from me when there are other teachers who are more qualified and experienced. Regardless of these reservations, I continued, cheered on by my family and friends. Both excitement and anticipation built as I prepared to launch my studio in a big way.

The Launch and Results

In the early stages of acquiring new students, aka capturing leads, my satisfaction came as I experienced their progression and growth with them. I discovered new skills and talents I did not know I possessed, and these talents came out more and more as I continued to teach more students. I learned that my teaching skills are right up there with the other great music teachers in my community and that I am both competent and capable of running a successful music studio. My students' joy became my joy, and so at times, I would ask myself, "Where else would I be able to find such impactful work as this?" The answer is simply nowhere else.

My day now consists of choosing my hours, organizing my business to be efficient and effective, spending the majority of my teaching time being blown away at how awesome my students are doing, and watching them experience the joy of progression. I wouldn't trade teaching for any other job out there. I realize that I can provide a service to my community that impacts people's lives in an incredibly positive way. I am providing my students with a learning environment that allows them to flourish in their understanding and playing of music, as well as an opportunity for them to express themselves through music.

In conclusion, why exactly did I capture the lead? In short, because it brought me joy. My own piano teacher's impact on my life is now magnified as I share what I learned from her with my students. I carry on this meaningful legacy and am honoured to do so. Seeing yet another student experience growth and fun in the process of learning to play an instrument that I love so much brings me so much joy, and that is worth it.

And so, I ask you, would capturing a lead provide the means to help another student along their musical journey? Could it provide you, the teacher, with the joy that only comes from watching someone else grow? Consider your worth and value to each student and may you be guided on your journey to help music pass from one generation to the next.

Author Bio:

Ray Ross – Piano Teacher – Performer – Expert Private & Group Class Instructor. Ray provides a multi-disciplinary lesson structure to allow students access to many styles and genres with a fun, relaxed, confident, and progressive approach to learning the piano.

https://prairiepiano.ca/

A TEACHERS MUSICAL JOURNEY

Leanna Minnick
USA

B orn in Canada, I spent my childhood in New Zealand, where I contracted the European measles at the age of six. My mother kept my older sister and I in a quiet darkened room to avoid complications. However, measles left my eardrum tissue extremely thin, and my eardrums ruptured, causing hearing loss. I would not realize how severe my hearing loss was until much later as I was a happy child who listened attentively when spoken to. My parents didn't notice my hearing difficulty. I had always loved to touch the wood of the piano and feel the rhythms in my soul when my mother would play. As my hearing began to fade, this became even more important to me.

We moved to America in the summer of 1959. Education at that time was further along in New Zealand and I went from four months of second grade, straight into fourth grade. When winter came, I saw snow for the very first time. The North Island, where I lived in Auckland, New Zealand, never gets snow. I was so excited to play in the fluffy white snow, throwing snowballs, having fun - but snow got into my ears resulting in painful earaches. My uncle was visiting and said it was wax build up causing my problem. He suggested pouring hot lemon oil in my ears to release the pressure. I screamed the moment that hot oil flowed into my inner ear. I never stopped crying and screaming from the pain until they gave me a sedative at the hospital that evening. The next day was the first of many operations in a period of about two years. Both the pediatrician and the audiology specialist were shocked at how much damage the measles had caused.

In fifth grade, in spite of the fact I had a hard time hearing, my father brought home a violin and said I was to learn to play it. I was so excited and happy to have my very own instrument. My teacher was a violinist in the Utah Symphony. He was so patient with me. However, I was not progressing as fast as others in my school orchestra because I could never tell if I was on pitch or not. It became a mathematical challenge to place my fingers in the exact same spot on the neck of my violin for each specific note. I learned to listen to the harmonies and loved being selected first chair in the second violin section of my school orchestras throughout the years. I continued to play violin in my school's orchestras for nine years. I loved it. Performing in the orchestra pit for school productions, such as *Guys and Dolls*, *The King and I*, and *Miracle on 34th Street* was such an influential and exciting part of my young life. It was during these years that I had the opportunity to learn other instruments. I was twelve years old, in seventh grade, when my mother discovered a Russian lady had moved into the neighborhood and was teaching piano lessons. Hence, several siblings and I began piano lessons. I realized very quickly that this teacher was not the kind of teacher I would ever want to emulate. She spent more time preparing dinner, answering the phone, and tending to her children while supposedly teaching piano lessons.

Two years later, when my two younger brothers were given accordion lessons, I picked up their accordion and played the piano and violin pieces I was learning. As I played the instrument, I could feel the sensation I felt in my younger years when I touched the wood of our piano while my mother played beautiful music.

When I was fourteen, I begged and begged my parents to allow me to learn another instrument. After six months of accordion lessons, I was on my way to California to compete in the Accordion Federation of North America Competition. The director of the studio coached me not to be disappointed, explaining that I would not earn a trophy having less than a year's study. I proved them wrong. I earned a fourth place trophy. Even though my hands shook like a violinist's tremolo while playing my solo, I did it. It felt amazing. When we returned home, I was asked if I would like to teach at the studio. So began my journey as a music teacher.

Being deaf, I taught myself to lip read. I sat on the front row of my classes and excelled in school and music academics. I looked in the faces of my young students as I taught and shared my knowledge and love of music with them. I wanted to be the best teacher I could be.

It was many years later that I realized how deaf I really was. I was married with young children at the time and one day we all went to the state fair. There was a booth offering hearing tests. Curious, I stepped inside. During that hearing test, I heard sounds I'd never heard before. I remember asking the audiologist, "Does everyone hear what I'm hearing right now"? I was stunned when I realized my own deafness. It would be many years before I would acquire hearing aids.

In 1990, while attending the University of Utah as a music major, I obtained my first set of hearing aids. Wow. What a difference it made. My professors were surprised I had chosen music as my major especially since I'd expressed I had never heard the sound of rustling leaves before. It reminded me of Beethoven, whose story struck a chord in me the first time I heard it in a music history class. Beethoven, at the premiere of his ninth symphony, was physically turned around to see the audience applaud him because he was deaf. That is why I loved playing the accordion so much, I could face my audience, see their delight and appreciation when I performed.

As I reflect on my journey, I realized at an early age, it's a teacher's responsibility to instill that great love of music. My deafness created many challenges for me in my life, but it also set me on a path to become a better music teacher and realize my full potential. Seeing, feeling, and hearing music has been a lifelong journey. I have overcome my handicap and I know the beauty and sounds of music are felt in the soul.

Author Bio:

Leanna Minnick, NCTM - National Certified Teacher of Music, UMTC Elite Educator, International Piano and Theory Teacher with a degree in Composition from the University of Utah.

https://musictheoryplus.online

26

AMAZING ANNIE OR INADEQUATE IRENE

Caroline Joy Quinn
USA

S ome would say I have captured the lead. Known as an expert performer, a sought-after teacher, published composer and arranger, best-selling author, course creator, mentor, and counselor, my life might seem almost perfect. Few would guess that I struggle internally. To be honest, at times, my struggles threatened to stop me in my tracks and steal my joy.

Let's consider what it means to capture the lead internally. Although this may seem like a strange topic, please stay with me as we explore the roles our inner voices play in enabling us to capture the lead externally. Does it matter which voice captures the lead? Why? This is my story. I didn't grow up feeling confident. Seen as quite ordinary, I understood ordinary people needed to be satisfied and to stop wasting time dreaming my life away. But I wanted more. Why did I work so hard longing for success? The answer is simple: I needed to prove to others that I was extraordinary.

All of us struggle with conflicting inner voices. One of my voices, nicknamed Amazing Annie, exudes confidence and joy. Alternatively, Inadequate Irene, constantly reminds me that I might fail and to set my goals accordingly. Which internal voice did I allow to capture the lead? Depending on my circumstances, the answer is both. This is what happened.

Years ago, no longer striving to meet the expectations of others, I found the courage to follow my dream of studying music therapy. After being accepted into a program, a very anxious, scared skinny, yet hopeful girl, boarded a plane alone to start a new life. Nothing was ever the same again. Three years later, I received my accreditation as a music therapist, and joined the rehab team at the Hugh Macmillan Medical Center in Canada. I blossomed in my dream job. My work using the technique of songwriting in a therapeutic setting with patients suffering from head injuries received national recognition. The next adventure was being the Head of Music in a middle school in Oxford, England. Four years later, settling in Seattle, music continued to be my world. Despite grueling life challenges, Amazing Annie did not let me quit. Through the years, and tears, she constantly inspired me to find strength and meaning in my teaching.

When asked to write a chapter sharing my journey as a music teacher, I was thrilled beyond words. Writing had been on my bucket list, and this was a golden opportunity. Did my dream come true? Not right away. Days after submitting my application, I was completely overwhelmed and swamped with feelings of inadequacy. What was I thinking? I hadn't written anything in years. Listening to others, I battled enormous insecurities leaving my mind muddled spending weeks rewriting instead of trusting my heart. What happened? For several reasons, my story was not chosen. My dream now seemed far out of reach. Processing this loss, Inadequate Irene seemed to be capturing the lead reminding me to have more realistic expectations. Maybe she was right. But the story wasn't over. Thankfully, I was given another opportunity to submit a new chapter. Wow. This time, listening only to my thoughts, I poured out my heart sharing many rich experiences writing like there was no tomorrow. Drum roll please. I am now an international best-selling author (twice) in an anthology dedicated to encouraging others in their musical journeys.

Why do I continue to strive to listen to Amazing Annie? Because being ordinary is not an option. I want to continue to capture the lead. I know that life is too short to let a fear of failure cripple me. But sometimes this is easier said than done. Seeking to grow professionally, I recently completed the Ultimate Music Theory Certification Course adding a fresh dimension to my teaching. Was it a smooth ride? Absolutely not. Despite outstanding course material, taking exams has never been my forte, and, once again, Inadequate Irene threatened to derail my progress.

Convincing me that I could fail the final exam, my notes were whisked out of sight. Over two weeks slipped by. Amazing Annie was beyond disgusted, and I knew she was right. Was I really going to let all my work go to waste? Definitely not. It was time to get back on the horse and finish the ride. Shortly afterwards, I wrote the exam passing with first class honors. Step by step, I have achieved more than I could ever have imagined, and now, I am teaching my students to listen to their empowering voices. When lacking confidence, as their coach, I can relate to their insecurities and together we persevere until they find success. But there are tough times too.

Sadly, relapses happen. Like many, I have experienced shattered dreams and depression as life events ripped my heart apart. Overwhelmed at times, I still listen to my unhealthy voice. Why do I work hard to get back on track? Because the alternative leads to spiraling down fast. I desire to live my life with gratitude. Gratitude and insecurities are not compatible. Praying and listening to inspirational music along with creating daily margins for rest and exercise are invaluable steps leading to recovery. And struggles are never wasted.

We, as music teachers, can choose which internal voice will capture the lead. One voice compels us to try new ideas, learn new skills, explore different styles of music, push through the discouraging times, reach out for help, and never give up. The other traps us into believing ordinary is fine, and change is scary, insisting there is no need for more growth personally or professionally.

Even as I am writing this chapter, the voices are still there. One voice is limiting, the other, freeing. Our voices, and choices, determine how far, and how high we will fly in our teaching and in our lives. Which voice will you choose?

Author Bio:

Caroline Joy Quinn, ARCT, Bach. Sacred Music, Accredited Music Therapist, Children's author, Piano Teacher and UMTC Elite Educator. She is a Composer, Arranger, Course Creator, Publisher, Mentor and Real Estate Broker.

https://www.linkedin.com/in/caroline-quinn-78575a42/

27

TEARS OF JOY - A VERY DIFFERENT CHRISTMAS

Glory St. Germain
Canada

Christmas has always been a time of celebration with family and friends, but little did I know what massive tears of joy would flow when I experienced *a very different Christmas.*

As my birthday is on Christmas Day, every year my parents would share Bible stories of the birthplace of Jesus in Bethlehem. Born into a musical family, it always brought me tears of joy as we would play music together to celebrate Christmas. My big dream had always been to travel from Canada to Bethlehem and experience God's Blessed Land for myself.

Can dreams come true? Little did I know this dream included thousands of people, one lost magician, and a broken guitar (sounds like the making of a country song).

In 1976, I was a young piano teacher - in love with the nationally recognized television star, recording artist, singer/songwriter, and legendary entertainer Ray St. Germain. In fact, his proposal to me was "I don't want to spend Christmas without you, will you marry me?" YES, I married the guy.

I may have started in the music business as a piano teacher, but after marrying into the entertainment world, my role became more - much more. I became Ray's booking agent, TV Show assistant, radio promotions hustler, and everything in between.

This would lead me to one of the greatest challenges of all, capturing the lead in booking the renowned overseas tour to entertain the Canadian Armed Forces in Germany, Israel, and Cyrus. Producing a show with twenty-four entertainers including a big band, Vegas style dancers, magicians, a mime artist, singers, MC, makeup/wardrobe, and headliner - all under our company Ray St. Germain Productions.

This was a huge opportunity, and I was up for the challenge. After spending months contacting musicians, writing contracts, and collecting promo material, it was finally time to submit my beautifully packaged proposal. And then it happened. The letter I had been waiting for. I was so excited to rip open the envelope. But as I read the first sentence, I was in shock. "We regret to inform you that your proposal has not been accepted." My heart sank. I'll admit it, I cried out loud. All that work, all my dreams, felt like they were for nothing.

Why?

I stared at the globe sitting on my desk, spinning it around to see the other side of the world where I wanted to bring this amazing show. I knew it would bring joy to the troops missing

Christmas with their families, so I submitted again the following year (with fingers crossed) and waited.

Several weeks later, the phone rang. It was The Major and he said, "Hi Glory, Congratulations. You are the first music producer in Manitoba to successfully submit an Entertainment Package proposal to perform for the Canadian Troops overseas."

Tears of joy ran down my cheeks as I screamed with gratitude. I shouted to my husband Ray, "We got it. We're going on tour." It was a joyful moment when I called each of the performers giving them the great news and started planning rehearsals in preparation for all the shows in Germany, Israel, and Cyprus.

The year 1983 would be a very different Christmas as our two young children David and Sherry would be staying behind with my parents. My dad happily read them the same Christmas Bible Stories he had told me. Sharing the pictures of Bethlehem where I would be visiting on Christmas Day. One of our older daughters, Catherine, would be traveling with us as she and her band The Rage were part of the show.

As we flew by Hercules aircraft, our first stop was Lahr, Germany. That's where we lost our magician Brian Glow. Traveling by bus to the base, we stopped at the bank to exchange our money. Everyone got back on the bus except for Brian (who was in the manager's office talking about the exchange). Yes, I was the leader of the pack, but it was like herding cats, trying to get twenty-four performers back on the bus and I forgot to count heads (Yes, only twenty-three heads got on the bus.).

At the reception a few hours later, we gathered to have a meet and greet with our wonderful hosts. About an hour later, Brian walked in. He told us he had one heck of a time taking a cab and even doing a few magic tricks to get past the checkpoint at the base, proving he really was a magician. After that, I always made sure to count heads.

The adventures continued as we then flew to Israel. We landed in Tel Aviv and started to unload the Hercules aircraft when, much to my horror, my husband's beloved ovation guitar came off with a crack down the middle of it. It had been laid flat when loaded with luggage piled on top of it. This was a gift I had given him complete with his name engraved on it for this special occasion. Unplayable, it would simply become a prop and later become part of his display in the Canadian Country Music Hall of Fame.

As the performers took the stage on Christmas Day, I not only felt pride in my accomplishment in capturing the lead in this industry but more importantly the tears of joy and a very different Christmas we brought to thousands of men and women whose lives we impacted with our music in the overseas shows performed in Dec. 83 - Jan 84.

As I look at the plaque hanging on the wall, it reads: Presented by The Royal Canadian Regiment to Ray St. Germain Productions - Glory St. Germain Producer, January 3, 1984.

I finally got to visit the birthplace of Jesus in Bethlehem. Tears of joy streamed down my face as I experienced a very different Christmas - a treasured memory. What impact did it have on my husband - the headliner? When we arrived back home and were reunited with our children and family, Ray went on to write and record another album entitled *Show Me The Way To Jerusalem* because we had all experienced something different.

Why set your goals to achieve something different? Why not?

Today, as a Music Teachers Business Coach, and Course Creator, my dream is to help you achieve your goals. For more information on our Ultimate Music Teachers Coaching Program - Contact us at UltimateMusicTheory.com and let's make your dreams come true.

Author Bio:

Glory St. Germain is an International Bestselling Author in *The Power of Why* Musicians Series, fifty plus *Ultimate Music Theory* books, Speaker, Coach, and Course Creator of UMTC Elite Educator Program.

https://UltimateMusicTheory.com/

AFTERWORD - THE 3 MAGIC KEYS TO DRIVE POSITIVITY INTO YOUR LIFE

Glory St. Germain

Everyone experiences stress in their life at some point. Sometimes we feel it is such a dilemma that it can be overwhelming, but only if we let it.

To live your dream and capture the lead in achieving your goals, consider the 3 Magic Keys to drive positivity into your life. These 3 keys can have a major impact on how you feel about yourself, your goals, and your outcomes.

The first Magic Key is the Key of A.

Whether you choose A Major, or a minor that's up to you. A is for ATTITUDE.

In fact, in order to drive positivity into your life, you need #PMA. Positive Mental Attitude. The way you deal with situations is a direct reflection of your attitude.

The Key of A has two choices, Major or minor, so do you have two choices about Attitude.

Think about your relationships in achieving your goals. You have a choice to show up with a PMA attitude, be a role model of what a Positive Mental Attitude looks like, even if you are not happy, or something has happened in your day to upset you. Live with gratitude for all the joyful things you have in your life, and that's the Key of A. Attitude.

The second Magic Key is the Key of B.

Whether you choose B Major or b minor, that's up to you. B is for a Beautiful State or B is for a Bad State.

If your relationships are not going well, or you feel like they are in a Bad State – play the game #turnitaround.

So how do you play "Turn it Around"?

You have the choice to turn any situation around. If you meet with someone who is in a bad mood, you can either get annoyed and simply get to work or you can #turnitaround with your PMA.

They will thank you for turning their day around. Perhaps they are having major problems in some areas of their life and feel like it's just the last straw. You have the key to turn their state from bad to beautiful and renew their faith in the fact that good things can still happen for all of us.

Now that you have the Key of A – Attitude with PMA, and your Key of B – Beautiful State it's time for the third key.

The third Magic Key is the Key of C - Communicate

The Major Key of C is to Communicate with Certainty that your message is clearly understood #solutionsonly. As musicians, we know about the interpretation of musical compositions, which is the same when interpreting emails, text messages, or any other form of communication.

When the written word is all we have, we need to choose our words carefully so they will not be misunderstood. #solutionsonly Sometimes we need to use emojis and happy faces to be sure we are understood.

When speaking to someone on the phone, smile while you

are talking. You may not think that they can "hear" your smile, but when you communicate with certainty and clarity – they can feel your heart.

The minor Key of c is to complain. What exactly does complaining get you? Nothing. It doesn't solve anything, in fact, it may take away all your keys to drive positivity into your life and you are back to square one.

As you decide which keys you want to implement into your life, remember You have a choice. You are the creator of your own destiny. Choose wisely.

Live by the 3 Magic Keys to drive positivity into your life to achieve your goals - Success comes with Attitude #PMA in a Beautiful State to #Turnitaround and Communicate #Solutionsonly with clarity. Here's to your success. May all your Magic Keys drive positivity into your life.

Live with Positivity.

ALSO BY GLORY ST. GERMAIN

The Power of Why 21 Musicians Created a Program
The Power of Why 23 Musicians Crafted a Course
The Power of Why 25 Musicians Composed a Legacy

ABOUT THE AUTHOR

Glory St. Germain ARCT RMT MYCC UMTC is the Founder/Author of 50+ Books of the Ultimate Music Theory Program and Founder of the Magic of Music Movement. She is on a mission to help 1 million teachers create a legacy through their businesses. She is the host of the Global Music Teachers Summits, Course Creator, Expert Music Teachers Coach, Publisher of the *Ultimate Music Theory* series, and an International Bestselling Author in *The Power of Why Musicians* series, an anthology of global authors/musicians sharing their stories of inspiration.

She is the founder of the UMTC ELITE EDUCATOR PROGRAM - A Business Accelerator in knowledge and expert strategies for teachers to use in order to run their successful music studios. She empowers educators to elevate their income, impact their teaching, and build their expert music business while enjoying personal time for self-care, family, and pursuing other passions.

In addition, Glory is an NLP Practitioner (Neuro-Linguistic Programming) and has taught piano, theory, Music for Young Children for over twenty-years, and contributed as a composer. She has served in various leadership positions to support music education organizations.

Glory has spoken on many international stages presenting workshops and is passionate about enriching lives through music education.

Glory loves learning and especially loves books on business and psychology. Mindset is a subject she believes has the potential to change our outcomes. Mindset is limited only by our own thinking. She is a Positive Mental Attitude Advocate and strongly believes that we need to see mindset as a priority, not only for ourselves but also for how we help others think, learn, and grow.

She is married to Ray St. Germain, a professional multi-award-winning entertainer and Canadian Country Music Hall of Fame inductee. They have five musically talented children, many grandchildren, and the family continues to grow.

Glory lives her life with gratitude, passion, and serving others through her work.

https://UltimateMusicTheory.com

ACKNOWLEDGMENTS

I want to thank all the musicians for being willing to share their stories of inspiration and most importantly their Why.

Their Why became the driving force that compelled them to stay the course, to never give up, and ultimately led them to capture the lead in their industry. I am grateful to them and proud to share the *power of why* their dreams became a reality in this book.

I want to thank my "UMT Dream Team" Shelagh McKibbon-U'Ren, Joanne Barker, and Julie-Kristin Hardt who helped me to implement these ideas and share them with the world.

Thank you to the hundreds of musicians, entrepreneurs, teachers, and students that I have learned from through the years who gave me the framework to build my company, write the Ultimate Music Theory Program, UMT Courses, UMT Membership, and compile the *Power of Why Musicians* book series.

Special thanks to our editors Wendy H. Jones and Lisa McGrath for their guidance, expertise, and countless hours in making this book possible.

It is with gratitude to everyone who has taken the risk to dream big and follow their heart to become a musician, composer, educator, or entrepreneur, and generously leave their legacy by enriching lives through music education.

Made in the USA
Coppell, TX
19 November 2021

66006870R10075